Contents

Teapot Hall at Dalderby, Lincolnshire – a survival of the early 'all roof' style of building.

TRACING THE HISTORY OF HOUSES

Bill Breckon & Jeffrey Parker

With Illustrations by Pip Challenger

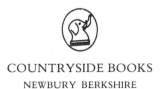

COUNTRYSIDE BOOKS

NEWBURY BERKSHIRE

First Published 1991
© Bill Breckon & Jeffrey Parker 1991

COUNTRYSIDE BOOKS
3 Catherine Road
Newbury, Berkshire

ISBN 1 85306 128 X

Illustrations by Pip Challenger

Produced through MRM Associates Ltd., Reading
Typeset by Acorn Bookwork, Salisbury, Wilts
Printed in England by J.W. Arrowsmith Ltd., Bristol

Introduction

England's architectural past is a particularly rich one and some of the finest old buildings in the world are to be found here: great palaces, imposing country houses, inspiring cathedrals and monumental public buildings.

But our architectural heritage extends far beyond the mere expression of pomp and power by Church and State, or a reflection of private affluence and civic pride. For in almost every town and village, and around every other corner in the countryside, there are further evocations of earlier times and of the people who lived in them. Not the rich and the famous, but rather the ordinary citizens – the farmer and the clerk, the craftsman and the merchant – living in their everyday houses.

These Englishmen's homes are still to be seen everywhere, some plain and simple, others elegantly appointed and elaborately decorated. Mellow medieval timbers for example remind us of the richness of the wool trade, sweeping Georgian terraces the beginnings of the Empire. In the countryside a village row of cottages may reflect the changing fortunes of agriculture while in the town villas and terraced housing plot the progress of the Industrial Revolution.

The four sections of the book have different uses. The first puts the everyday house in historical context, charting the social, economic and political pressures that all contributed to making our old houses the way they are.

Since geography has also shaped our houses, Section Two gives information about the regional variations in building styles and materials – from the mud cob cottages of Devon to the fortified tower houses of the northern border country.

Section Three will help those who want to make a more detailed study of the basic components of a house. There is a wealth of information about the roof and the walls, about windows and doors and about floors, staircases, fireplaces and chimneys. Each chapter may be read right through, or the cross references from the previous sections can be used to identify passages of interest. This section should also be useful to those who live in older houses as it contains hints on repair, restoration and replacement. Owners of old houses will be aware that there are sometimes restrictions on what alterations can be undertaken. Restrictions apply for instance if a house is a Listed Building or if it lies in a Conservation Area.

Section Four will be particularly useful when you are out and about, enabling you to identify and date, with a fair degree of accuracy, the houses you come across in your travels. By answering some simple questions about the house in front of you, you will be able to 'home in' on its style, type and age. Houses very often do not remain in their original condition: they are altered, enlarged, improved, renovated, so that their outside appearance might well conceal a very different heart within. Only inside investigation or local records enquiries will reveal everything. Nonetheless this section will enable you to identify fairly precisely the face that a house shows to the world.

The houses around us are both a legacy of our past and a monument to our increasing technological knowledge which has enabled us to use new materials and more sophisticated building methods to improve our domestic environment. The study of old houses gives an exciting insight into the practical repercussions of economic and social change; detailed knowledge of these structural developments gives a new dimension to our study of social and local history.

However you use this book, whether as a 'house-spotting' guide or a more detailed essay in history and building technique, we hope you will find, as we have, that the more you know about the everyday English house, the more you'll enjoy everyday England – in the country, in the villages and in the towns.

I

THE HOUSE
IN HISTORY

The aisled hall was developed by skilled Saxon timber craftsmen and was to form the basis of all the designs most commonly used for house building right through the Middle Ages. Later refinements included a raised dais for comfort above the earth floor and the partitioning of the end bay into areas of privacy, usually for the most important members of the household.

The Saxon and
Medieval Periods

Our earliest ancestors were nomadic hunters and, as such, did not build houses of a permanent nature. Later, the domestication of animals and the cultivation of crops led to a more settled existence and more permanent dwellings. When the Romans invaded Britain in 44 AD they brought with them advanced techniques in house building and town planning. The influence of these techniques affected the development of the local population's dwellings too and many an Iron Age farmstead eventually replaced its timber house with a modern rectangular villa as the focus for its agricultural life – first in timber, and later in stone.

TIMBER HOUSES

After the gradual breakdown of Roman organisation came the eventual emergence of a recognisable Anglo Saxon civilisation. The Saxons were skilled timber workers with the ability to square off large timber beams and to fix them firmly together with mortice and tenon joints secured with wooden pegs. The finest example of their skills is the 'aisled hall' house, a design for living which, with variations, was to be used right through the Middle Ages. By the 10th century it was said that England's wooden halls had no rivals anywhere in Europe – making everyday living fairly comfortable for the rich and privileged. The aisled hall is basically a series of bays, rectangular boxes of timbers on which the rafters lean. The Halls at Old Yeavering and near Cheddar were the largest timber buildings in a complex whose subsidiary buildings at Cheddar included a bakehouse, a possible ladies' bower, a cornmill and a private chapel, the latter built in stone. The side walls of the earlier halls were slightly bowed with the timber uprights for the walls set in a continuous trench; later the upright timbers were jointed into horizontal timbers – ground sills – set in a sleeper trench in the ground. Not only did this add strength to the structure by spreading the loads, it also helped to prevent damage by rising damp, since posts planted straight into the ground tended to rot more quickly as water seeped easily into the end grain. The gable end walls may well have been full height walls, made either of timber or filled with panels of wattle and daub, or, alternatively, lower walls may have supported a hipped roof. Inside, where twin rows of wooden pillars divided the living space into aisles there would have been a fire in a central hearth, the smoke from which escaped through holes in the thatched roof. The hall was the focal point for daily life where the whole household congregated, ate and slept.

Although a considerable advance in house design, the early Saxon Hall was still a relatively low and sprawling construction. As the centuries progressed, however, it evolved into a more finely proportioned building in which a number of refinements added to the comfort of the occupants. It became the practice, for instance, to build at the 'upper' end of the hall, away from the doors, a raised, paved dais above the mess of the earthen floor, and to partition off the end bay into cubicles to give the more important members of the household some degree of privacy.

By the 11th and 12th centuries the hall was often extended to encompass two storerooms at the 'lower' end – the pantry, for bread, (from the Latin *panis*) and the buttery, for drink, (wine and ale in butts). These were divided by a central passage running to a proper kitchen outside in which the cooking fire was now installed. In many houses, however, cooking was still done over the open fire in the hall.

STONE HOUSES

While timber formed the basis for the vast majority of English houses, by the end of the twelfth century a privileged few were able to have their homes built in stone. Stone building at first had been virtually the prerogative of the powerful leaders of church and state, and before the turn of the century almost the only stone buildings of note were the fortified residences of feudal overlords or the monasteries, religious foundations and churches built for rich and influential ecclesiastical authorities.

By 1200 or so, though, the first great phase of church and castle building had slowed and some masons were released to sell their skills to others able to afford them.

A fair number of the private houses they built still exist, and are generally known at King John's Houses, since many originated in his reign. By modern standards they are by no means imposing, seldom bigger than 20 ft wide and 40 ft long, but with their two-storey elevation and their solid stone walls, they were the envy of their day.

Many were the town houses of rich merchants, while others, built in

The Normans brought new stone building techniques to England and by the end of the 12th century some rich and influential citizens had their homes built of stone. A few still survive today and are generally known as King John's houses as many of them were built in his reign.

the country, were probably attached to a timber hall. Living accommodation was on the upper floor – known as the solar – which was usually of stone, supported on vaulting from the floor below. The vault below was used for storage, particularly of valuables, and was generally only accessible from above by an internal staircase. The upper storey was reached from the outside by a flight of stone steps. (In some of the town houses, however, the lower floor was used as a shop or workshop, and could be entered directly from the street). The best example of a group of these town houses are the so-called Jew's Houses in Lincoln, built at the end of the 12th century.

Another form of upper floor living was the tower house, where again, the main living area was on the first floor, with further private rooms and bedrooms on a second, and even higher floors. A spiral staircase, sometimes built within the thick stone walls, sometimes contained in a projecting turret, linked the storeys. Again the ground floor was used for storage.

Upper floor houses and aisled halls, however, were very much the exception, not the rule. For most people in the 12th and 13th centuries –

and for the poorest, for the artisan and peasant right up to the 16th century – home remained the rude, crude hut of rough poles lashed together and thatched with turf or heather, bracken or straw. None of these dwellings survive today. Indeed it seems that they were constantly being rebuilt and that their owners did not expect them to last much more than a lifetime. Archaeological excavation shows that the circular

Cruck building is an ancient building technique. Crucks, pairs of curved oak timbers set some 16 feet apart were baulked and jointed to make an arch which formed the main supports of the roof. The crucks were strengthened with tie beams, joined with purlins, and for greater stability a collar beam was usually inserted a few feet from the apex. Cruck houses usually had walls of wattle and daub panels or cob. In the 15th and 16th centuries the introduction of brick or stone chimney stacks enabled the upper part to be floored over to create an upper storey. Timbers large enough for this type of construction became scarce during the 17th century and cruck houses were rare by the 18th century, only being used for smaller houses as timber allowed.

form of hut, with its wigwam of lashed poles, coexisted beside and then gave way to the rectangular plan, with rafters leaning on a ridge pole. The simplest would be just one big room, with the smoke from the fire in the central hearth escaping through a hole in the roof. Sometimes the family and their animals shared it at night. Low walls could be built to raise the roof a little, but higher walls had to be of more complex construction because of the pressure caused by the outward thrusts of the rafters.

Two solutions to this problem emerged, and began to give many ordinary houses the outline that we would recognise today. They are the cruck, and the box or timber frame.

Crucks

Crucks are large pairs of curved or angled timber baulks jointed together at their tops to form a rough arch. Each cruck vaguely resembles a massive shepherd's crook and in fact both words have a similar origin. By using pairs of crucks as the main supports of the roof, the interior of the house is opened up. No longer is it all sloping ceiling; instead an open, arched cross-section replaces the cramped triangular cone.

Cruck building is an ancient technique and although its origins are obscure it was certainly used in pre-Norman times. It began to be really popular, however, in the 11th and 12th centuries and was to continue to be used as late as the 18th century.

Crucks at first formed the basis of large and small house alike, but in later centuries they were to be found mainly in smaller houses, the box or timber frame being favoured in larger ones.

The geographical distribution of cruck houses has long fascinated the historian, for they are to be found in Scotland and Wales but have been identified in England only to the north and west of a line running roughly from Flamborough Head to Southampton. It is uncertain why this should be so: some historians believe that cruck houses were originally constructed all over England but were replaced in eastern and south-eastern areas by more advanced building techniques. Others suggest that they never spread from the north and west because the south and east were more accessible to, and influenced by, continental countries like Holland, Germany and France, where crucks were never used.

Whatever the truth, crucks certainly proved a practical and straightforward method of constructing a better-proportioned home, and they were much prized.

Cruck houses were, like the Hall, built in bays, each pair of curved supports being set some 12 to 16 ft apart, and the size of the house was defined in title deeds and building contracts – and for taxes – by the number of bays. A typical cottage would be only one or two bays long while the more substantial house would have three of four bays, with the familiar domestic arrangements of central open hall section flanked at one end by the private family rooms and at the other by the pantry and buttery. Walls would be made of panels of wattle and daub, or cob, which was popular in northern areas. The introduction of the brick or stone chimneys in the 15th and 16th centuries enabled the upper part to be completely floored over. (For details of construction see p 136.)

Box Frames

In the south and east particularly, another solution to the headroom problem was emerging: that of box frame (often called timber frame) building. With this technique fresh skills are required to cope with the problems of containing the downward pressure and outward thrusts of the roof supports and covering. The roof has to be trussed, that is held or tied together by some internal arrangement of jointed timbers.

The basic module for a timber frame house is a rectangular open box of solid timbers, similar to the supporting bays of the aisled hall. But now the rafters are supported on the wall-plate, the top beam of the side wall section, and prevented from splaying by the internal trusses.

There were many variations of roof truss, and differing regional styles which owed more to local preference and tradition than to the strict application of scientific principles.

The box frame construction had many advantages over crucks, allowing much more flexibility in the ground plan of a house, and it could be built higher – to two full storeys if needed – but one of the drawbacks was that each truss needed a tie beam across it, to counteract the outward pressures. This of course meant an obstruction when the walls were still relatively low, or when an upper floor was incorporated. One solution was to replace the tie beam with a collar beam nearer the apex, but since this gave less support against the outward pressures extra beams, braces and struts had to be added. Some of the commoner forms of roof trusses are the crown post, king post, queen post and arch-braced collar-beam roofs together with one of the great glories of medieval timber building, the hammer-beam roof. (Details are given in the chapter on Roofs pp 69.)

As with the cruck, the use of box frame technique meant that at last houses could have higher walls. The sturdy timbers of the frame took the weight of the roof so the walls were not load-bearing, and the space

The box frame construction represented an advance in house building which was developed throughout the Saxon and Norman periods. A box of solid wall timbers took the weight of the roof rafters and so the walls were not load bearing. This allowed more flexible interior arrangements and enabled the house to be built higher, with two storeys if needed.

between the timbers could be filled in with wattle and daub panels, brick nogging or clay blocks. (Further details in Chapter on Walls p 94.)

While the new techniques of timber construction were beginning to provide better houses for those of more modest means, major design changes were also afoot for the great halls. Here too, timber frame, and to a much lesser extent cruck, building had raised the roof and provided taller side walls. But further additions were to make the hall not only a place for communal living, but a proper home for the family as well, with much more privacy and comfort. This was to be achieved by combining house and hall, building onto the single-storey original a double storey at right angles.. Some of the surviving stone King John's Houses were additions to halls, but it was also common practice to build these extra wings in timber, or as hybrids, with a stone lower storey and a timber-framed upper one.

The family could now escape from the hurly-burly of the communal Hall to their own rooms, and particularly to the solar, the upper floor of the adjoining wing. A further development was to have not just one extra wing but two, so that the roof of the hall was now flanked with two other roofs, running at right angles to it.

In the south-east of England in the 14th century a new style of house evolved that rationalised these combinations by putting them all together under a single roof. It is called the Wealden house or Yeoman's House, although neither term is strictly accurate since such houses were neither invariably inhabited by yeomen nor confined to the Weald, being found as far north as Yorkshire and as far west as Devon.

The Wealden house

The Wealden house owes its origins to the demands of a new class of Englishman emerging in the 14th century. The Black Death in mid-century had killed more than a third of the population and, with the shortage of labour and consequent peasant troubles and uprisings, settled arable farming had become difficult, if not impossible. Many farmers, great and small, turned to sheep, an enterprise that was to prove highly profitable and to form the basis for England's prosperity for centuries.

There was a thriving export business, too, which particularly benefited those who lived in the south-east, with easy access to the Continent. So in counties such as Kent and Sussex there was a new breed of richer farmers and businessmen, in social status and wealth midway between the peasantry and the hereditary nobility. These newly-rich yeomen and merchants demanded something much better than the hovels of the peasant. They wanted houses that echoed, albeit modestly, the great halls of the lords their parents and grandparents had served.

In concept the Wealden style, which was to become a standard design for two centuries, resembled the double-ended Hall: a central Hall, open to the roof was flanked by end rooms on two storeys. But now all was contained under one roof and the end rooms on the upper floors extended outwards on jetties. This jettying technique was to be much used in Tudor times and the various reasons put forward for its introduction are discussed in the next chapter.

Wealden houses usually had a hipped roof of thatch, although in more Northern areas gable ends are not uncommon. Generally they were well-timbered, with the wall studs placed closely together. Another characteristic of the design is the arched braces that run across the front of the hall section, from the side of the upper rooms to the roof, supporting the eaves.

The rooms at one end of the house were used for service – pantry and buttery below with a storeroom, or perhaps an extra bedroom, above. The use of the rooms at the other end depended very much on who was living in the house: a merchant, for instance, might have used the

16

ground-floor room for entertaining. Originally known as the bower or even simply as a chamber, this room was eventually called the parlour, from the name given in monasteries to the room where visitors were received. The room above, the solar, was reserved for sleeping. Farmers, on the other hand, and especially where married sons and daughters were living in, often used this lower room as a bedroom too. As with earlier hall houses, there was usually a cross-passage screening the service rooms from the hall, with access from an outside door. When the hall section was only one bay wide, the passage would be contained in the service rooms themselves.

Particularly fine examples of the Wealden house are The Old Shop at

The Wealden House style emerged in the late 14th century when many farmers and merchants, newly rich from the prosperous English wool trade, built modest sized versions of the halls of the gentry. It became a standard design for two centuries most commonly found in Kent, Sussex and Surrey. It consisted of a central hall, open to the roof, flanked by end rooms on two floors, the top floor extending outward on jetties. Jettying adds an endearing quality to these houses especially as carpenters liked to show their carving skills on the exposed joist ends. Early Wealden houses were thatched. In this example, 'Synards' at Otham in Kent, the central hall has been floored over and a 17th century dormer window inserted in the new upper floor.

Bignor in Sussex, and Synards at Otham in Kent, but although the design features of such houses were fairly standard it is sometimes difficult today immediately to recognise them. Invariably the hall has been floored over at a later date and chimney stacks added. That presents few identification problems, but other restorations and modernisations may have heavily obscured the original outlines. For instance, it is not uncommon for fresh ground floor walls in brick or stone to be built up flush with the jettied overhanging walls of the upper storeys, a practice often carried out because of decay in the original timbers. But inside, evidence of the earlier wall can usually be found in surviving timbers and in the mortice holes where the original studs were tenoned in; these will be one foot or more inside the line of the present wall. The unglazed mullioned windows will often have been enlarged and new windows inserted in different positions, and the outside 'look' of the house may be disguised by rendering or by tiles hung over the timbers. These additions and alterations mean that no-one is really sure how many Wealden houses still remain after four to six centuries but undoubtedly there are hundreds. A fair number of them are now museum pieces, having been dismantled, restored and re-erected on sites open to the public (at the Open Air Museum at Singleton in Sussex, for instance.)

Initially Wealden houses had been relatively cheap to build in the well-timbered areas of Britain, but by the 16th century wood was becoming much scarcer and the fashion for them gradually died away. It is important again to remember that only a very small proportion of the population in the 14th and 15th centuries could afford to live in such comparative splendour. Nonetheless, the growing wealth of the country in late medieval and Tudor times led to an increasing demand for better houses and to what has been described as the Tudor building boom.

The Sixteenth Century

The period from the closing years of the 15th century until the beginning of the 17th century saw increasing commercial success for England, and a substantial population explosion – from less than three million people to more than six million. Small wonder that it was a boom period in house building. The prosperous middle classes wanted to extend their existing properties or to replace the shabbier ones. Thus homes built of, say, cob, were pulled down and spanking new houses put up, built in stout oak, in stone, or in the latter part of the period, in brick which was by then coming into more plentiful supply.

The 'Great Rebuilding' required armies of carpenters, masons, brick-layers, daubers, thatchers and tilers, all highly skilled men who had served a vigorous apprenticeship and who were proud of the greater freedom and respect that their skills had brought them.

Not all the houses being built, however, were of solid and superior construction: the smaller cottages built for the poorer members of the burgeoning population were more often than not flimsy affairs and just about all of those built before the 16th century have long since perished. The period houses which we today call 'cottages' are invariably the former homes of the richer yeomen. In most of England (particularly in southern and central areas) these houses were built in the village, for it did not become the custom for farmers to build isolated farmhouses on their own land until much later. Their houses would have been looked on with envy by their poorer neighbours whose homes were often hastily erected, since a man was allowed to build on common land, provided that, starting at sunset, the house was sufficiently completed to have a fire burning in the grate at dawn. So many such hastily-erected homes were built that it caused official concern over the encroachment of common land, and in 1589 a law was passed to try to control such building.

The swelling ranks of skilled craftsmen were nonetheless providing great numbers of well-built houses which still stand sturdily today in our country villages and towns and, to a lesser extent, in the cities (where they have been more often replaced). Most of the wealth of the country was concentrated in the south, so it is in this region that most examples

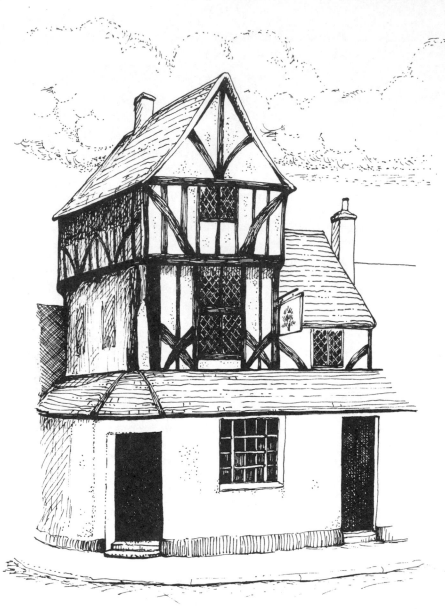

Building land was at a premium in towns in the Tudor period, and houses began to grow upwards like mini-skyscrapers. This three storey example at Thame, Oxfordshire, is now the Bird Cage Inn.

survive. It was in the south too that innovations in design and building techniques generally started. They spread only slowly to the rest of the country: it could take as long as a century for new ideas fully to permeate the more isolated regions in the north. For this reason a house in the south-east of similar design and construction to one in, say, the north-west may well have been built up to a hundred years earlier.

As we have seen, the box frame was very much a southern style, while cruck frame construction was most popular in the north. Box frame construction, with their greater flexibility, spread slowly northwards and probably hastened the decline in cruck building, which had petered out by the end of the 18th century, the last such houses being built in the Lake District.

The Fireplace and Chimney

Two interrelated factors significantly affected the internal arrangements of English homes in the Tudor period. One was the demise of the large open Hall that had originated in medieval times. Its end was hastened by the need for more and better accommodation, more individual rooms within the house. The other factor was the advent of enclosed chimney stacks, replacing the open hearth.

Early attempts to overcome the problem of smoke-filled rooms, using hoods and flues of wattle and daub, had been unsatisfactory, not least because of the fire hazard. The very well off, and those fortunate to live in areas where stone was readily available, could have chimneys made of it, but these were comparatively rare, and it was not until bricks were being produced in quantity that the chimney became an integral part of ordinary homes. Its introduction meant that the upper part of the open hall was now smoke-free, so a floor could be put in, providing a two storey house. At first chimneys were installed in, or added to, outside walls, but later the fire was placed centrally again, with the chimney emerging through the middle of the roof. This new arrangement required more sophisticated joinery techniques to butt the upper floor around the chimney.

The need for more rooms and the introduction of the central, enclosed chimney stack meant a radical departure from the medieval concept, which had held sway for generations, of a house as hall, parlour and service rooms. Now the upper storey – or storeys, for the timber frame house, especially in towns, was growing ever taller – became devoted to bedrooms, a convention that remains to this day.

The central stack also meant that back-to-back fireplaces could be installed bringing warmth to two rooms. Those on the ground floor could thus be used for the purpose that best suited the household. A common arrangement was to build the chimney in what had been the screens passage dividing the hall from the pantry and buttery. These, now heated, became new parlours, sitting and dining rooms. The old parlour, more often than not, would be relegated to a service room. An alternative design placed the chimney stack between parlour and hall, with fireplaces to heat both. Whichever the arrangement, it was also found that a convenient space was created between the stack and an adjacent wall in which to build the staircase.

Chimneys rapidly became status symbols, so much so that it is not uncommon to find Tudor houses with more chimneys than there are rooms: this was the owners showing off to the neighbours. Much skill was lavished, too, on the design and decoration of the stacks where they emerged from the roof. Among the most pleasing are those in spiralled and patterned brickwork. Many originals survive, although not a few were built in Victorian times, to Tudor design.

While the bricklayers were showing off their new-found skills, the carpenters too were revelling in their ancient ones, and a wealth of fine detail and elaborate carving, both inside and out, was a characteristic of Tudor and Elizabethan timber buildings. The carpenters were not economical in their use of wood: much more was used than was strictly necessary for structural reasons and wood was extensively incorporated for purely decorative effect, such as in close vertical studding for the walls and in the marvellous 'magpie' work of the west Midlands and the north-west. This elaborate form of decoration is based on a series of rectangular panels, each containing diagonal wooden strips or curved braces to form an overall geometrical pattern. The design is heightened by blacking the timber and whitening the plaster in-fill. Fine examples are to be seen in Chester and, perhaps the most famous of all, at Little Moreton Hall in Cheshire.

In the towns, constrained by their ancient protective walls, land for building was at a premium, and the Tudor builders tried to solve the problem, as have their 20th century successors, by building upwards. Creaking and unwieldy-looking houses soared to four, five and even six storeys. They were invariably jettied, each storey over-hanging the one below. This certainly provided more space on upper floors but its popularity was more likely dictated by fashion rather than function. Those jettied Tudor mini-skyscrapers that still remain in our towns have often lurched and become deformed by time, showing how difficult it was to build high and be really secure using a timber-frame technique.

As well as the Great Rebuilding, the 16th century also saw much

Brick became a very popular home-building material during the great rebuilding of the 16th century, especially in Kent, Surrey and Sussex. The innovation of the enclosed chimney stack made it possible to have more private rooms within the building and meant a radical departure from the medieval concept of living accommodation.

renovation and alteration: notably in the replacement of windows. Narrow unglazed medieval mullions were taken out and bigger glazed windows put in. (The process was to be repeated a couple of centuries later when the windows of many Tudor houses were replaced with Georgian ones.)

In the country, too, it was a time of change and reconstruction and such change would have been particularly noticeable in England's 'highland' zone of the north, midlands and south-west. We have seen how in the middle and south of the country the yeoman farmers usually built their homes in the village, venturing forth each day to cultivate their separated strips of arable land. The few isolated houses in this country-

23

In timber buildings in East Anglia, and particularly in Suffolk, it became fashionable to cover both the timber and the wattle and daub panels with plaster. This was then scored and combed into decorative patterns, or moulded into shapes and designs. This technique was called pargetting (from the French *Par* – all over, and *Jeter* – to throw). The fashion for pargetting was at its height from the late 16th century through the 17th, and fell from favour during the mid 18th century.

side would be medieval manors, extensively modernised. In the 'high-land' zone, however, the 'long' house, standing on its own, had been traditional for generations. It enabled those keeping livestock, to be in closer touch with their flocks and herds.

One long roof sheltered both a narrow house, one room deep, and the byre for the animals. In this period of prosperity, however, the animals were ousted from the end of the house to separate quarters in the farmyard, and the original byre was converted to living accommodation. More often than not, with the addition of a chimney, it became a proper

24

kitchen. Large numbers of long houses were so converted, and they can often be recognised by difference in the basic structure at what was once the byre end, where less care was originally taken in building.

Sometimes the byre continued to be used for animals but access from the house was sealed off. Such buildings are called 'laithe' houses, from the local word for byre, and are found mostly in Yorkshire.

By the end of the 16th century and increasingly in the early 17th, good timber was becoming scarce, not just because of the demands of the building boom but also because the best wood was needed for the ships which were so important in the country's commercial success and expanding trade. Over the years the amount of wood put into houses decreased, close-studding for instance disappearing and magpie work declining. Inferior, misshapen and irregular timbers were often used and there seems to have been a distinct fall in craftsmanship, too, for beams and posts were built into the frame in an almost haphazard way. It is easy to identify many early 17th century houses by the diagonal timbers in the walls, now necessary additions to give some stability to the weakened structure. Second-hand wood was often used and cheaper, softer woods replaced oak.

The fashion for jettying, so uneconomical in timber use, soon died out and, since large curved baulks were so scarce, cruck building became impractical in all but the smallest houses.

The Seventeenth and Eighteenth Centuries

The seventeenth and eighteenth centuries were to see further great changes in house design, both in town and country. In the town, a major disaster prompted legislation which was to alter the whole appearance of the urban scene; in the country, legislation itself enforced a new way of life, which led to disaster for many.

The look of our towns was altered by the Great Fire of London and the Building Acts that it engendered; the shape of the countryside was changed by the Enclosures Acts which overturned centuries-old agricultural practices.

Town Planning

For centuries kings and parliaments had issued edicts, formulated laws and drawn up regulations to try to minimise the ever-present risk of fire in England's crowded towns. With so much timber used in house construction and with haphazard check-by-jowl building, the towns were packed to their walled seams and were veritable tinder-boxes. One small spark could lead to a major conflagration. All the laws, edicts and regulations, however, had little effect, as was so dramatically demonstrated not only in London's Great fire of 1666 but in other, earlier infernos, such as those that had gutted the centres of Bury St Edmunds and Northampton.

The risk of fire – and disease too – were further compounded in the 17th century by a considerable increase in speculative building. Most earlier houses had been built to order, the builder's client becoming the occupier. Now the speculative builder was putting up 'off the peg' homes, for sale to anyone who cared to buy during or after construction. Without the intimate relationship between customer and constructor it was inevitable that corners were cut and standards lowered to maximise profit. It was not just a London problem and although the laws enacted generally referred to the capital, they were taken up by other towns and cities. In 1605 James I had decided that action was needed and banned any fresh building in timber in London: only brick and stone were to be used.

But the regulations, and other controls introduced in subsequent Building Acts, were largely ignored, such was the demand for new houses. The speculative builder continued through the first half of the century in his bad old ways, building cramped and unsafe houses both within and outside the city walls.

The Great Fire of London not only brought about fresh laws but also it seems, a change in attitude, for the Rebuilding Act of 1667 was for the most part observed. One undoubted factor in its success was in the tighter control of building practices on site, by official building inspectors appointed to examine the work as it progressed and make sure the minimum standards were being met.

The 1667 Act and those that followed it in the next century changed the appearance of our towns and cities by specifying standard types of houses that could be built, and by relating the size of the house to the width of the street. It is interesting that the builder of this period, no longer able to indulge private fancy in overall design, increasingly used ornamentation around doors and windows to give some stamp of individuality to his building. The 1667 Act, like earlier laws, referred specifically to London but its commonsense technical provisions were adopted by many other towns and cities and the new uniformity of style spread countrywide.

The Act laid out with a fair degree of precision four types or 'sorts' of houses that were allowed to be built. Terraced houses predominated to make the best use of limited space, and the first, and smallest, sort of house described was two storeys high, with cellar below and attic above. It was decreed that the principal rooms had to be no less than 9 ft high, and the cellar and attic at least 6 ft 6 inches. The thickness of the walls was laid down too: two bricks thick to the first floor, one-and-a-half up to attic level, one brick thick to the roof.

The shape and appearance of towns was further regulated by provisions governing the width of the streets. These 'first sort of houses' were the only ones allowed in the narrowest streets, 14 ft in minimum width, sufficient to allow two carts to pass each other. In broader streets, of some 18 to 24 ft 'the second sort of house' could be built: one of three storeys, with attic and cellar if desired. Again there were regulations on ceiling heights and wall thicknesses, as there were for the 'third sort of house', imposing four-storey dwellings which were to be set in the few main streets of 30 to 40 ft wide. (The 'fourth sort of house' was one set in its own grounds and its shape and size were similarly regulated.)

All these rules and regulations obviously affected the outward appearance of the house, enforcing a simplicity and a symmetry unseen in the higgledy-piggledy Tudor and Elizabethan town. But throughout the seventeenth century other influences had been at work too, notably the classical ideas seeping across from post-Renaissance Europe. Particularly influential was the work of Andrea Palladio who adopted classical styles for use in domestic architecture and whose book was translated into English in 1676. The great architects of the day – such as Inigo Jones in the early part of the century and Christopher Wren in the latter half – influenced domestic architecture through the imitations of their styles and details seen in great private houses and in public works. Jones was also innovative in pushing the idea of having architect's drawings made of the house before its construction. In earlier periods the contract between customer and housebuilder would seldom have contained drawings.

From the builder's previous work the customer would know roughly what the house would look like. Such vagueness was no longer appropriate in the 17th century where, with standardised shapes and sizes, it was the refined detail that was most important. Hence the need for drawings. Some classical details had already begun to appear in Tudor and Elizabethan times but as the seventeenth century progressed they were to be seen more and more, in pediments over the front door, for instance, in decorative mouldings and around the windows, and on cornices, parapets and balustrades concealing the roof, and pilasters stretching from ground to eaves level. Also influential in the overall 'look' of the house was the sash window (see chapter on Windows p 119.) which tended to make window proportions taller and relatively narrower.

The decline of the traditional housewright, who might take six months to complete a one-off house, and the rise of the professional architect, who might produce fresh designs in as little as six days, meant that ideas were to travel, and could be copied, much more quickly and the new styles of building spread rapidly across the country. In stone-and-cob building areas there was less change, due mainly to the limitations of the materials, but even here minor echoes of the new styles were to be seen: in keyed brick-work lintels and doorway dressings in stone-built houses for example.

The constraints of the new building regulations influenced the internal arrangements of the house too. Each floor usually contained two rooms, the front room running the whole width of the house while the rear one was narrower to accommodate the staircase. The passageway from the front door made the front ground floor room narrower too, so the grandest room in the house was the first floor front, and it became the principal living room. In the third sort of house particularly, this room

The introduction of the classical style of architecture in the 17th century with its clean symmetrical lines marked a complete departure from the timber-framed houses of the previous centuries. Rows of well-proportioned windows and an imposing central front door were major design changes which were to set the pattern of house styles for the next two centuries.

was further enhanced by the addition of a balcony, some 4 ft wide, which as well as adding to the aesthetic appearance also helped to inhibit the spread of fire from below. These balconies and their balustrades were a focal point for decoration, especially when ironwork came into plentiful supply, and they remained principal features of town houses well into the 19th century.

One of the remarkable consequences of the building regulations of the latter part of the 17th century was that different social classes lived in similar types of houses, the only real difference being in size. It it true, however, that the smaller types of house tended to be less well-built than the larger ones – and in many city areas they quickly degenerated into over-crowded slums, with the sort of social life depicted in Hogarth's 'Gin Lane'.

In the Country

While 17th century legislation created new styles for town housing, later laws of a very different nature forced substantial change in the country. The 18th century Enclosures Acts literally altered the shape of the countryside, and the farmhouses and cottages in it. Until then the pattern of agriculture had hardly changed for hundreds of years and the countryside looked very different from today's patchwork of fields. Husbandmen eked out a living from separate strips in large open fields, a piecemeal system that was far from efficient: agriculture struggled to meet the growing demand for food from the swelling populations of the towns. Eighteenth century governments determined to do away with the strip system and to create larger and more efficient units. Enclosure by agreement had been happening since the 13th century but the 18th century Enclosure Acts completed the process with undue haste. The increased interest in cattle-breeding and the keeping of large herds also prompted legislation to enclose land to prevent animals straying, an expense beyond the pocket of many smaller farmers who were forced to sell out. Field and pasture were enclosed by fence, hedge and ditch, altering the look of the land and bringing about devastating social change. Loss of common grazing for his animals rather than the actual act of enclosure ruined many small husbandmen. The husbandman might have been poor, but at least he was independent, and even those hands who worked for more prosperous yeoman farmers (owning more holdings) enjoyed a close relationship with their employers, in whose house they ate and often slept. Now the enclosures evicted many a smaller farmer to starvation or to seek work in the towns. The new generation of farmers, with larger domains – and greater profits – introduced new, larger-scale systems of agriculture changing old working practices and losing in the process the old communal spirit to a much more formal boss–and–worker relationship.

The newly-rich farmer also wanted a better type of house. In most of England he had previously usually lived in the village: now he was to build a new house on his own land, dividing up his old village dwelling into cottage 'rows' to accommodation his workers. These are the terraced cottages so common in our villages and they can usually be recognised by the one long communal roof, with the major chimney stack of the original dwelling now accompanied by several smaller stacks from the new fireplaces put in to heat each sub-division. Interestingly, with the reduced demand for labour in today's modern, mechanised farms – and the increased demand by farmworkers for better housing – these small cottages are often no longer required and many have been converted back into a single house, reversing in the 20th century the processes of the 18th century.

Quite a few of the farmhouses whose owners had been ruined by the enclosures became alehouses, dispensing some alcoholic comfort to the rustic workers, and many a country pub owes its origin to these days. Others along village streets, had their parlours converted into shops.

The new houses the farmers built on their own land were much squarer in plan than the long, one-room deep village home. Those few older isolated farmhouses that remained were often completely rebuilt, or the best parts of them incorporated into the new house, usually forming a rear kitchen wing behind the finely-proportioned rooms of the Georgian addition.

GEORGIAN PERIOD

The classical style of architecture gained popularity in the late 17th and early 18th centuries. It reached its zenith in the late 18th and early 19th centuries – the Georgian period.

The rambling nature of earlier large country houses had given way to the much more compact and rectangular plan, and to a house with clean and symmetrical lines, especially on the facade, where rows of well-proportioned windows were balanced about an imposing front door set firmly in the centre. In the big house, medieval and Tudor details were replaced with classical ones and there were major design changes, such as the superseding of the gabled roof by the hipped one – and the roof was often hidden behind a parapet. The hall declined still further in importance, no longer being used as a living area but merely an extension of the entrance, although often none the less grand for that. The staircase, which had been earlier usually tucked away, became a prominent feature and its emergence often ousted the single large fireplace from its central position, replacing it by smaller ones serving individual rooms.

The smaller country house, like those for the farmer, the parson and the squire, reflected the style of its imposing neighbours, notably in becoming two rooms deep, rather than one.

In this typical Georgian 'double-pile' plan the service rooms and kitchens occupied the back of the house, while the main living rooms graced the front. The bedrooms were on the first floor. Its depth did, however, create technical difficulties, for a greater span had now to be roofed over. One early solution was to construct the roof in the shape of an M, with a gutter in the central valley, or with a flat lead section between the two ridges. The heavy tiles first used required a high-pitched roof, but with improved transportation brought about by the digging of the canals, Welsh slates became available and a lower pitch was possible. This meant that the roof could now be covered in a single span. Mansard roofs became popular at this time too, their shape allowing additional attic rooms.

In the towns, when there was space available, similar Georgian double-pile houses were built, often two and sometimes three-storeys tall, with additional attic and basement. In the latter were now to be found the kitchen and the service rooms, releasing those on the ground floor for living or for business (ideal for the doctor or the local solicitor).

The facade usually had five sash windows on the upper floor or floors, and four on the ground floor, divided by the central doorway, which had a classical hood or pediment or a projecting pillared porch. The towns were becoming even more crowded, however, so such double-fronted properties tended to be built more in their outskirts. Towards the centre, the lack of space and the legacy of narrow medieval building plots meant that Georgian re-building was usually of the terrace type, often just one room wide and two deep, with the doorway set to one side of the front windows.

Of course, Georgian development was not confined to central re-building or to larger homes in the suburbs. With increasing industrialisation and trade the towns were expanding fast and a prosperous middle-class was also demanding new homes *a la mode*. The speculative builder was again hard at work, buying up or leasing tracts of land (usually outside the confines of the old city walls) and laying out squares and circuses, parades and terraces of well-proportioned houses that combined to provide a harmonious whole. The spas, like Bath, and the seaside towns were among the leaders in such developments, but they were to be found everywhere – and most are still in use today. In fact more than a million Georgian homes, it is estimated, are still inhabited.

Brick was by now the most popular building material, although stone was still used where it was available, and timber-framing building continued, too, although this was always either rendered and scored to imitate stonework, or weatherboarded or hung with 'mathematical tiles' which mimicked brickwork.

The countrywide uniformity of style, imposed by the constraints of the Building Acts and the demands of classicism in determining the proportions and features of the house, was generally pleasant but it did lead to a certain amount of drab uniformity.

Such changes in fashion as there were related more to detail and decoration than to alteration in basic structure. Styles changed slowly through the 18th century and the greater variations are to be seen in the superior town and country houses rather than in the more lowly terraces. Among the changes of note are increasingly detailed pediments over

Early Georgian homes made use of ashlar stone as a building material. The introduction of sash windows and a shallow pitched roof, often hidden behind a parapet, gave them their distinctive appearance. As in this example, blind windows were a feature, sometimes to avoid window tax, but more often built in as an integral part of the symmetrical design of the frontage. The plain glazed sash windows shown here are uncommon. The classical style of six pane double sashes were most often used.

doors and windows, more pronounced pilasters with highly-decorated capitals and the introduction of temple-like recesses, with or without accompanying statues. Windows changed subtly, to, with panes generally becoming larger and glazing bars thinner. The three-section Venetian window, with its tall, rounded central part was also a later introduction.

REGENCY STYLES

The Regency period at the end of the 18th and beginning of the 19th centuries saw the addition to the classical lines of the Georgian style of many curious overseas influences. As Britain extended her interests abroad, so the early Empire-builders brought back ideas from distant

As towns expanded during the 18th century, terraces of well-proportioned houses were built to accommodate a fast-growing population. These were often three storeyed. Door and sash window surrounds became more ornate and ironwork decorations became fashionable on balconies, as windows embellishments and railings. As in this example, from the mid 18th century, it became common to apply stucco over the brick construction to resemble the cream-coloured stone so fashionable in the new Spa towns like Bath.

Egypt, India and the Far East; ideas that architect and designer melded into the classical framework. There was a vogue for chinoiserie, for the odd sphinx or two sitting somewhat incongruously on pillared facade and, with shades of Mogul India, the Hindu style, whose apotheosis is the delicious Brighton pavilion.

Another distinctive characteristic is a lightness of touch and a delicacy of detail. Now that most large towns had at least one iron foundry, decorative ironwork was increasingly used in staircase, balcony, window embellishment and railing. The larger foundries published catalogues of the designs that they were mass-producing, in panels of standard widths to be strung together to enhance any size and shape of balcony or window. Among the best known was the Carron company of Falkirk whose work may be seen all over the country and whose 'hearts and honeysuckle' pattern was used by the Adam brothers at the Adelphi in London and much copied elsewhere.

While much of the Regency effort was directed towards superficial decoration, rather than alteration in house shape and size, this period did see the introduction of the bow window, previously largely confined to shop front. The bow often ran the whole height of the house and, from shallow beginnings, deepened into a well-rounded curve towards the end of the period.

The treatment of the row of terraced houses as one architectural unit reached its zenith in the Regency, in the symmetrical perfection, for instance, of the Royal Crescent in Bath and in John Nash's terraces around Regent's Park in London. The spas and seaside towns were booming as the fashionable sought some fresh air and 'took the waters' – salt or otherwise. Bath and Brighton continued to dominate but others, such as Leamington and Cheltenham among the spas, and Sidmouth and Weymouth at the seaside, were popular too and have been left a legacy of pretty Regency Houses.

From the mid-18th century onwards there was a widespread use of stucco, applied over the brickwork and often coloured to resemble stone, cream being especially popular since it resembled the much desired Bath stone. Nash used it to blend his terraces into a single architectural whole and the Adams favoured it too. Their clients, and all those who wanted 'better' houses were also undoubtedly influenced by the fact that exposed brickwork was now increasingly to be seen in factories and in humbler homes.

Stucco had a further advantage because although the Georgian and Regency house would invariably look impressive, all was not necessarily as it should have been. The building boom, and speculative development particularly, had led to a lowering of standards. The demand for bricks was often met only by using those made of unsuitable clay, insufficiently fired to withstand prolonged attack by the elements. Builders also cut costs by using mortar with too little lime in it and with much of the sand replaced by dust from the road. To encourage the mortar to set, fires were sometimes lit against the walls, but even so many of them were quick to crumble. Stucco could, and from mid-century onwards frequently did, cover such shortcomings and of course it provided some measurement of protection from wind and rain.

THE GOTHIC REVIVAL

Despite the splendour and harmonious proportions of classical architecture, or perhaps even because of it, in the second half of the 18th century a reaction began to set in. There was a desire for novelty and change and a hankering for the romantic and the picturesque in both art and architecture. There was also, it seems, a need for reassurance, for some links with the past, as the Industrial Revolution brought about rapid change both to the social structure and to the landscape. A growing interest was kindled in the ruined remains of ancient abbeys and castles, often now painted by artists and visited by fashionable coach parties, and the rich built mock ruins and follies on their estates. The new-style light reading, the novel, often had a medieval setting: two notable examples being *The Old English Baron* by Clara Reeve and Horace Walpole's *The Castle of Otranto*. All this inspired an interest in medievalism and in the architectural details of the 14th and 15th centuries, which began to be added with an almost careless abandon to houses of all shapes and sizes.

Horace Walpole himself was a pioneer of the new fashion, in his small Georgian house at Strawberry Hill near Twickenham, bought in 1750, to which he added all sorts of medieval excrescences – tower and battlements, pointed Gothic windows and moulded Tudor chimneys. This exuberance gave its name to a new style of architecture: Strawberry Hill Gothic.

The gothic (or Gothick – the extra 'k' distinguishing its early phase) revival was at first a sprightly and lighthearted affair, the builders competing with each other to provide medieval details for their clients. The gable-end made a comeback, with bargeboards often fretted and decorated; windows were made with the pointed gothic arch, tracery patterns and leaded lights; dripstones and mock battlements could be bought 'off the shelf'. There was little regard for historical accuracy in the early period of the revival, for the builders had scant knowledge of the evolution of medieval building systems and, in the absence of masons, were quite happy to recreate mock-gothic details in wood and plaster. These were added piecemeal to conventional Georgian houses of all types, with no attempt to return to the houseplan of medieval days.

Classicism was not dead, however, and a counter-attack was mounted, particularly in the introduction of true Hellenistic architectural styles, based first-hand on actual Athenian examples rather than the second-hand versions that had come from Rome, via the Renaissance and the influential designs of Palladio. For decades there was a battle of styles, and home-buyers could look through the builders' pattern books to choose gothic or classical details as the fancy took them.

The Nineteenth Century

The gothic revival of the second half of the 18th century was given further impetus in the 19th century by the historical novels of Sir Walter Scott, with their detailed descriptions of medieval settings. The later styles, however, were much more sombre and serious-minded than the light-hearted fun of Regency times. Now builders and architects were trying to reproduce historically-accurate copies of medieval styles rather than merely add gothic details. Half-timbering came much into favour, with the panels between the beams filled with herringbone pattern brick nogging or with ornamental plasterwork. 'Leaded lights', with hexagonal patterns and elaborate handles and catches, were turned out *en masse* by the iron foundries. Tile-hung facades were popular too, and chimneys were invariably tall, with twisted shafts in moulded brick. The gothic revival was also much in evidence in churches, where it helped to reinvigorate ancient crafts such as the making of stained glass and ornamental floor tiles. These found their way into domestic architecture – the well-endowed parson often being a promoter of the new styles in his own home – with stained glass in half-glazed doors and in bathrooms, and ornamental tiles in halls.

ARRIVAL OF THE SUBURBAN VILLA

Much of this medieval detail was also to be seen in another type of house, the suburban 'villa' being built for the growing numbers of industrialists, merchants and professional men, to reflect their social status and wealth. The term villa had earlier been applied to the finely-proportioned renaissance-style houses built by the country gentry in the 18th century. By the 19th however, it was being used to describe these new properties, usually built in the suburbs, within easy reach of factory, mill or office. Set in its own grounds and fairly compact in plan, the suburban villa had most of the principal ground floor rooms interconnecting, while kitchen and other service and utility rooms were usually placed in an abutting wing.

Some villas were built in good-quality brick but in others inferior brick was used and the imperfections covered over with stucco, often elaborately decorated. The battle of styles continued, with gothic and romanesque and mock Tudor vying with the classical. There was an increasing heaviness and solidity in style, a rejection of the lightness and frivolity of the Regency, almost as if there was an unconscious realisation that there was no place for such *joie-de-vivre* in this mechanical, industrialised age.

One result of industrialisation was the production of large sheets of glass, so that now the window space could be filled with large panes, unbroken by glazing bars, save for the horizontal bars of the sash. Inside, the fashion was for high ceilings, with moulded cornices and elaborate ceiling roses, from which, as the century progressed, were hung gasoliers, as town gas replaced oil and colza lamps for lighting. Thick wallpapers abounded, and much of the interior timber was painted in dark colours, in imitation of old and expensive woodwork. Floors, too, were of wood, covered by a thick central carpet, and mahogany rails were popular for the main staircase. The overall effect was somewhat sombre.

HOUSING THE NINETEENTH CENTURY POOR

The price of the rapid material progress which allowed the rich industrialist and aristocrat their unparalleled luxuries was paid by the poor. They lived in conditions little better than those of their medieval ancestors, and in the over-crowded towns especially, arguably a good deal worse.

The towns were expanding rapidly as the dispossessed and the desperate crowded in to seek work. In London, for example, the 1851 census counted an increase of 330,000 or 17 per cent more than in 1841, and some smaller towns more than doubled their population in a decade.

The late 18th and 19th centuries saw hundreds of thousands crammed into town centres, living where they could – whole families to a room in older houses whose former occupants had left for the comforts of the suburbs; or crammed into ill-lit insanitary dwellings thrown-up by speculative builders. Around the gaunt new factories that fuelled the Industrial Revolution grew a labyrinth of mean streets, row upon row of dingy, slate-roofed back-to-backs.

An early form of cheap mass-housing was the court – a huddle of shoddy buildings grouped around a small, open central area.

One such court, in Portman Square in London in the 1840s, was surrounded by 26 three-storey houses, in which no less than 914 people lived. Its only drainage was a single sewer. Small wonder that diseases such as cholera and typhoid, were rife, and death a constant companion. The houses around courts were built back-to-back, that is, they shared rear external walls, and had no back doors. This technique was used, too, in row upon row of cheap terraces which were particularly to be seen in industrial towns from the 1830s onwards.

But if conditions were hellish for those in the towns, for many who stayed in the country they were almost as bad. Those for whom there was still work on the land often endured accommodation hardly better than that for the livestock. Some shared the converted longhouses abandoned for new farmhouses by their employers; others lived in hovels built of mud, all of which have since crumbled away.

There were, however, occasional chinks of light in this gloomy picture of England. A few enlightened landlords had seen fit to provide decent homes for their labourers, either through philanthropy or in a tidying-up and landscaping exercise on their estates, demolishing old homes and building new well-planned villages. Early examples include Nuneham Courtney in Oxfordshire and Milton Abbas in Dorset, both built in the second half of the 18th century. Some enlightened industrialists, too, had earlier provided better homes for their workers, notably the Strutt family in Derbyshire, who, again in the late 18th century, built solid stone houses at Belper and at Milford for the workers in their cotton mills. There were to be further such developments as the 19th century progressed but even so for the average agricultural labourer or factory worker and for the millions packed into the towns, dirt, squalor, disease and death were to remain the norm for the most of the century.

The better-off largely ignored, or were seemingly unaware of, the problems of the poor. It was not until mid-century that the national conscience was properly roused, through the exposures of such writers as Dickens and the activities of campaigning reformers, like Octavia Hill. The upright were also appalled at the immorality of the masses which they believed stemmed mainly from the dreadful conditions in which they were forced to live. Respectable Victorians were becoming worried too about disease: human waste often seeped into and polluted the water supplies and cholera and typhoid were no respecters of social status, a fact that became conspicuous when Prince Albert died of typhoid in 1861.

Much of the early work to provide better housing was undertaken by charitable trusts, such as the Metropolitan Association for Improving the Dwellings of the Poor, which built the first block of family dwellings in Stepney in 1849 and for which the Prince Consort himself had helped design a model tenement block. Another notable name was George

Peabody, an American who had settled in London and who gave half a million pounds to raise the blocks of Peabody Buildings, many of which still stand today. Such 'flats' – the idea was imported from the continent – made tenement dwelling more respectable, and although today we may regard the blocks as grim and stark they were vast improvements on the slums they replaced.

BUILDING LAWS

The legislators were busy too, spurred on by each outbreak of cholera (which *The Times* called 'the best of all sanitary reformers') and forcibly reminded of the problems by the stench of the Thames – by the 1850s a putrid open sewer – which seeped into the new Houses of Parliament. So, in contrast to the buildings laws of the 17th and 18th centuries, which had concentrated on fire prevention and soundness of structure, those of the 19th were more concerned with health and sanitation. A series of public health and building Acts between 1848 and 1890 laid down requirements for drainage, waste disposal, refuse collection and water supply. Further, the Victorian legislators strengthened the powers and widened the responsibilities of the local authorities, most of which had been ill-equipped to deal with the overwhelming increase in their populations and the disastrous living conditions it had created. Local councils became directly responsible for public works of drainage and sanitation, and were empowered to raise money to acquire land, clear slums and build houses. Thus was born the era of council housing, a system which through the 20th century provided housing for a substantial proportion of the population, until the advent of 'the right to buy' scheme and owner occupation during the 1980s.

London had made an early start in slum clearance, destroying what has been called 'the disreputable and unsavoury rookery known as Porridge Island' between St. Martin's-in-the-Fields and Whitehall, and laying out Trafalgar Square (in which Nelson's Column was erected in 1843). During the latter half of the century many more such clearances were undertaken in many towns and cities. The 1890 Housing of the Working Classes Act added impetus to the policy of demolition and rebuilding by making loans available to local authorities. By the First World War, the very worst of the problems had been dealt with, although hundreds of thousands of houses and tenements, cramped and crowded and with inadequate lavatories and washing facilities, still existed. It has to be said that in many local authority schemes the new houses were not as substantial an improvement as they might have been: many of the new buildings were themselves to be condemned as slums later in the 20th century.

Victorian legislation brought fresh controls to the private sector, too, giving local authorities power to compel owners to make good unsound and insanitary property and also insisting, under the By-laws, on minimum sizes and standards for new housing. Private builders contributed to the Victorian rebuilding under strict controls. Hundreds of thousands of terraced 'by-laws' houses were built in the late 19th and early 20th centuries; sturdy little homes, 'two up and two down', with, if you were lucky, a kitchen at the rear and, if you were luckier still, a bathroom. Many thousands still stand and, if well modernised, continue to provide cosy and comfortable homes; others have fallen victim to the bulldozer and were replaced by the dubious advantages of the high-rise flats of the 1960s.

HOUSING THE NEW MIDDLE CLASS

The poor who suffered and the rich who enjoyed unprecedented material well-being were not the only two levels of Victorian society. There was a growing middle class of office workers, managers, shop-keepers, craftsmen and the like – respectable, hardworking and ambitious. It was they who, searching for somewhere more pleasant to live, with more space and fresher air, spurred on the development of the suburbs and heralded the age of the commuter. Their escape from the town and city centres was made possible by the development of the suburban railway system and by the tram and the omnibus.

Many lived in superior terraces, bigger and better than the squalid back-to-backs, often with a small front patch and a larger garden at the rear. A typical better-class terrace house had a narrow hall – uncompromisingly usually called a passage in northern England. Boxed-in stairs led to a narrow landing off which opened two bedrooms. Often a further staircase led to a single attic room lit by skylights. Of the two ground floor rooms the rear was the living room (with a kitchen beyond), while the front room, or parlour, was kept for best. Others living in the suburbs were able to proclaim a greater status by living in a 'villa', not now standing alone but semi-detached.

Whether catering for the villa owner – detached or semi-detached – or for the buyer of the superior terrace, the builder was able to offer housing in a variety of styles and treatments. Almost invariably brick-built and slate-roofed, Victorian houses came with all manner of embellishments in various styles: classical, romanesque or gothic. Windows and door-

While the rich Victorians favoured villas, and the poor were often housed in inferior back-to-back houses, the emerging middle classes of Victorian England discovered the suburbs. For them developers of the day built superior terraces with gardens back and front and a room for a servant in the attic area. These houses were invariably brick built with slate roofs, but architectural embellishments differed. This example favours the Gothic style, but classical or romanesque designs were equally common.

ways would be picked out with rendered pillars, lintels and arches, often with a coarsely-detailed keystone, or with their surrounds in different-coloured brickwork. Those palely reflecting the classical style would often have a flat lintel instead of the triangular pediment favoured by the Georgians. Details tended to be a coarser and plainer imitation of the current vogue in larger houses.

For the better off, the ornate – even overpowering – gothic style was still much in evidence. The combination of tall arched windows, often set in dark-red or greyish brick, under slate roofs of deep and varying pitches, imparted a sense almost of foreboding and this outside impression was matched by the sombre decoration inside: dark paints and papers and solid furniture. Many examples of these Gothic houses are to be found the North London suburbs of Hampstead and Highgate, previously outlying villages but swallowed up in London's sprawling expansion.

The bay window continued to be popular in all sizes of house, but instead of having a Georgian or Regency curve, it now became three-sided. The ground floor bay window often had its own slate roof, or it might continue into a first-floor bay, again topped with an individual roof.

The Victorian suburban medium-size house accurately sums up the aspirations of the age, and especially of the middle-class. It is increasingly solid and respectable, and shuns external flamboyance. It also reflects a growing uniformity, a lack of individuality, which the industrial age produced. Vastly improved transport systems, and factory-produced materials available from one end of the country to the other, meant that a Victorian house in Cumberland, say, would be much the same as one in Cornwall (different-coloured brick, perhaps, providing the only variety).

THE VERNACULAR REVIVAL

Mass production also brought about a decline in local skills and craftsmanship which wilted under the competition from usually inferior but invariably cheaper factory-made materials. Towards the end of the century there was a reaction to this, in the Arts and Crafts Movement and in the Vernacular Revival. The former, inspired by William Morris, demanded a return to honest craft, not only in the fabric and furniture for which it is most renowned, but also in architecture. The latter expressed a reaction against both the foreign formality of the renaissance and the excesses of gothicism. Both movements mirrored a similar reaction in the world of painting: that of the pre-Raphaelites.

These influences showed themselves in a brief return to the home-grown English styles of the Middle Ages and the ideas were particularly taken up by the new breed of wealthy business-men and industrialists (and their wives) who wanted houses built in the country where they could enjoy comfortably the fruits of their commercial enterprise as if to the manner – if not to the manor – born. The result was a peppering of the countryside with mock-Tudor and other reproduction houses, some entirely fanciful, others seeking to echo the styles of local houses centuries old. Some architects even produced houses instantly aged, with sagging roofs and apparent repairs, such as added and unnecessary buttresses to support walls. Mullioned windows, leaded lights and exposed timbers were again much in evidence, and although the overall effect in many such houses is pleasing enough, in others the combination in a single building of features from several distinct periods produces an architectural hotch-potch which verges on the grotesque.

The Early
Twentieth Century

Following the First World War there were few who could continue to have built or to run large and purpose-built houses (although architects like Edwin Lutyens were able to provide them for those who could) and the Vernacular Revival can really be counted the last full flowering of an individualistic building style in Britain. Its influence, however, has lingered on, notably in the still popular so-called 'cottage style' and in the 'stockbroker Tudor' residences built between the wars in the outer suburbs and the dormitory towns that surround our big cities.

Other late-19th century ideas continued to influence the 20th although their ideals have often been diluted, if not swamped, by demand for mass housing and the constraints of economics. In 1898, for instance, Ebenezer Howard published *Tomorrow*, promoting the concept of a 'garden city', in which the layout and the setting of large numbers of houses were as important as their individual style. In his scheme of things the city of the future would be a carefully integrated mixture of industrial development and housing, surrounded by a green cordon of farmland, the whole a pleasant and healthy place to live and work. Such large-scale planning had previously been given little serious consideration, but the success of the first garden cities – like Letchworth (started in 1903) and Welwyn (started 1920) – and of 'garden suburbs', like that of Bedford Park in West London (designed in 1876) and Hampstead (opened in 1907) helped to foster the concept of 'new towns' in which municipal responsibilities shifted far beyond merely providing new homes for the underprivileged to designing whole new communities. The New Towns Act of 1946 further fostered such development.

It is beyond the remit of this book to discuss the styles of building for the post war years of the 20th century, not least because this period has seen such diversification and confusion that little overall pattern can be discerned. But in the early years there was the occasional flurry of individuality, such as in the curved lines of the Art Deco of the 1920s and 1930s, but such recognisable styles-of-their-times have been few. Since then we have seen stark practicality, where function rather than form,

One of the last recognisable 'styles of its time' is that of the pre-war semi-detached, with its distinctive bay windows, sometimes with curved glass in the corner sections, in the Deco style.

was paramount, and neo-Georgian nostalgia, such as in the tall, thin town house, complete with ground floor garage; we have seen the spread-out council housing estates, and the identical boxes of private property development. We have seen, too, the high-rise flat, gaunt and forbidding, and a flurry of various vernacular styles in the property boom of the 1970s and 1980s.

Perhaps future generations will identify and select the best on offer for preservation and appreciation. Those of us seeking a home of charm and individuality, a house that reflects the needs and aspirations of those who live in it and tells us something of local skills, styles and materials, must look back over the centuries.

2

THE HOUSE
IN ITS REGION

Introduction

When we think of early houses – of the 15th, 16th and 17th centuries say – the picture most likely to spring to mind is that of the timber houses: the top-heavy, jettied check-by-jowl well-mellowed homes standing proud in the village or countryside.

Wood, however, was by no means the universal building material. The poor could seldom afford the substantial timbers needed to build a house that would last, nor the services of carpenter and wright. They made do with lowlier materials like mud and clay. And all around the country, especially where wood was scarce, even the better off used what was most easily to hand: stone, perhaps, or flints, or again, clay.

So there are distinctive regional traditions in building and localised styles that often continued for centuries, little altered by changing fashions. Such fashions, it is true, might influence the building of the great houses, where money and distance – for shipping materials – were no object; and details would certainly slowly seep into the smaller homes. But the appearance of many an everyday English house would for generations have depended primarily on its location, on the economic prosperity – or lack of it – of the regions, and above all on the building materials plentiful locally.

It was not until the 19th century, with the railways making brick and slate universally and cheaply available, that such regional variations began to disappear. Happily, in many of our towns and villages much evidence of earlier styles remains.

The main feature of the regional styles are outlined here, and further details of building materials and techniques are to be found in other chapters, notably those on roofs and walls.

Southern England

Travelling across southern England from Cornwall to Kent, it is easy to discern the overwhelming influence of locally-available materials: stone dominates in the sparsely-wooded far south-west, but moving eastwards mud and clay soon take over, to be replaced in their turn by timber-framing in the well-forested south and south-east.

The stone houses of the south-west, particularly Cornwall, are mostly built of granite. Although hard and durable, it is difficult to work, so while some of the better houses were built with well-dressed blocks, it was commonest to use rough-hewn stones, often with rubble in-filling. For straightness and strength however, dressed stones were used at the corners. Houses with dry stone walls are also still to be found in Cornwall. The difficulty in working the local stone accounts for the notable lack of carved detail in the ordinary houses of the area.

Mud-walled houses are so common in Devon that cob, the local term for the mixture of mud, grit and straw used, has come to be applied to the variations of mud-based walls found elsewhere in England too. Such houses were probably once common over the whole of the southern region but they have now practically disappeared in places like Kent, where people were later wealthy enough to replace them with timber and brick buildings.

With no supporting timber frame, cob walls need to be thick to hold up the roof – several feet thick at the base, tapering gradually towards the top. The most obvious characteristic of a cob cottage is its rounded corners and deeply-recessed doors and windows, which are generally few in number. The outside walls were protected against the weather by successive coats of limewash and the house was given 'a good hat', usually of thatch originally, although often replaced with slates. Devon and Cornwall incidentally saw the early use of slate as it occurs naturally in the region, the quarry of Delabole in Cornwall being a notable supplier. West country slate is still produced but the industry fell into decline when cheaper Welsh slates became more plentiful in the late 18th and early 19th centuries. In Cornwall the local variation of cob is 'clob', in which broken slate is added to strengthen the muddy mixture. Devon still has hundreds of cob houses and cottages and although few of those

A typical West Country cob cottage. Cob is the local name for the mixture of mud, grit and straw used for the walls. These houses are characterised by their thick walls, rounded corners and deeply recessed doors and windows. Usually, as this example, they are thatched but in Devon and Cornwall, there slate occurs naturally, some had slate roofs long before Welsh slate was readily available throughout England.

surviving are much more than 200 years old, the largest cob house in the county, Sir Walter Raleigh's birthplace at Hayes Barton, dates from the 16th century.

Both rough stone and cob walling place restrictions on the size of houses and often extra accommodation is provided by building extensions or 'outshuts', covered by a roof sloping almost to the ground.

The upland regions of Devon and Cornwall also saw the early development of long houses to shelter both the farmer's family and his livestock. Such houses were subsequently altered to provide extra living space, the animals being housed elsewhere. Other characteristics to watch out for are tall, tapering chimneys (to be seen particularly on Dartmoor and in Cornwall) and a large rounded projection on house fronts, which originally contained an oven.

In the counties of Somerset, Dorset, Wiltshire and Hampshire cob houses are again much in evidence although with subtle differences from those further west. The earth here contains more chalk, and the lime in this both helps hardening and gives the walls a white appearance. In Dorset, especially, local heather was substituted for straw in the cob mixture, while in the New Forest, in a technique peculiar to the area, walls were built of *pise de terre,* or rammed earth.

There is good building stone in these central southern counties too, and it is much easier to work than granite, so many houses built with well-dressed stone still stand, some surviving from as early as the 15th century. They can be built taller than the West Country cob cottages: two full storeys to the eaves compared with the one-and-a-half common in cob (half of the upper room's height being contained in the roof space). Dorset had brown limestone and dark grey Purbeck stone, much favoured in churches but used in domestic architecture mainly for roof tiles. Portland stone, used by Wren for St Paul's, comes from Dorset too, but it was little used locally, being too expensive and hard to work. Wiltshire has the milky Chilmark stone and Somerset, the famous Bath stone, richly creamy and used not only in building the 18th century heart of the town but on into the late 19th century as well.

In the Middle Ages this Central Southern section was well wooded, and as one moves eastwards there is an increasing preponderance of timber-framed houses. But whether the building was of timber or of stone, the usual roofing material was thatch. Although the high-quality Norfolk reed was sometimes used, the commonest material was a local variation of combed wheat, known as Dorset reed (for thatching materials and techniques, see p 72.).

Kent, Surrey and Sussex have long enjoyed prosperity and so still contain a wealth of fine old houses in timber, stone and brick, some surviving from the 13th and 14th centuries. These counties were originally densely forested and timber-framed houses of all kinds abound. Equally there are local clays suitable for brick-making, so some of the earliest brick-built houses in the country are here too, with particularly fine red-brick Tudor houses. (For an example of a red brick Tudor house see page 23.) There is stone to be found, too, notably sandstone around East Grinstead, Bargate stone and the pale Kentish Ragstone, seen particularly in the Maidstone area.

The Wealden house (full details p 16.) is probably the best-known house type of the area, but is only one of all manner of shapes, sizes and designs of timbered buildings to be found in the south-eastern counties. Generally the earlier the house, the more heavily-timbered it will be, for by the 17th century timber supplies were becoming scarce, not only because of the demands made by housing but also because so much charcoal was being made for use in iron-smelting, begun here in Norman times. Whether heavily or lightly timbered however, houses in the south-east tend to be plainer in decoration and more utilitarian in design than those in, for instance, the Midlands and the north-west.

Weatherboarding is to be found particularly along the Kent and Sussex coasts, where it was much used in the 19th century, both to cover up poor structural timbers and, merely because it was the fashion, even to overlay the fine exposed timbers of medieval houses. An alternative technique was to tile-hang the walls, making them very durable and weather-proof but giving a feeling of bulkiness to the property. Tile-hanging became a widespread practice in the 17th century as the new brickyards turned out large quantities of tiles as well as bricks. Mathematical tiles, imitating brick, are usually found only in Sussex, although it is unclear why this is so.

Although thatch was used in these parts, a more characteristic early roofing material was stone slabs, requiring heavy timbers to support their weight. 'Horsham slabs', from the quarries near the town, found their way over much of Sussex and are still to be seen, although unfortunately all too often the appearance of such fine old roofs has been spoiled (although the weatherproofing improved) by cementing-over. Tiled roofs are also common and are less steeply pitched than the stone ones.

Eastern Counties

The essential features of the typical old house in East Anglia and eastern England are timber-framing, external plaster and big chimneys. As in the south-east, early prosperity meant many good quality houses were built – and large numbers are still to be seen. The isolation of the area from the rest of England, until comparatively recent times, has also meant distinct regional styles, and the region was also subjected, perhaps more than anywhere else in the country, to continental influences, particularly from the Low Countries.

Suffolk is particularly rich in architectural history. Again once densely forested and especially wealthy in the Middle Ages with profits from the booming wool trade, it probably contains more fine timber-frame houses than any other county. They can be seen at their best in Lavenham, a village that has become a showpiece of medieval architecture. It was left largely unaltered after its rapid decline in prosperity at the end of the wool boom.

Most Lavenham houses have exposed timbers but during the 16th century it was common practice in Suffolk, and elsewhere in East Anglia, to cover both the wattle and daub panels and the supporting timbers with plaster. Mixed with hair and dung for strength, it could be scored with combs into decorative patterns, or to be moulded into intricate shapes and designs, in a technique known as pargetting (see Walls, page 98). Particularly good examples of this kind of work are to be found in and around Ipswich, notably The Ancient House there. The centre of Ipswich, incidentally, also contains some richly-carved timber houses. (For an example of a rendered timber pargetted house see p24.)

Many plastered Suffolk houses are pink in colour, this 'Suffolk Pink' being originally a mixture of whitewash and the blood of cattle. Nowadays those wanting to keep the traditional colours are able to buy paints and washes with less gruesome ingredients.

East Anglia also contains some of the earliest brick houses in England, a reflection of those continental influences, especially from Flemish immigrants who brought brick and tile making techniques over with them. They introduced new styles too, notably in the curved and

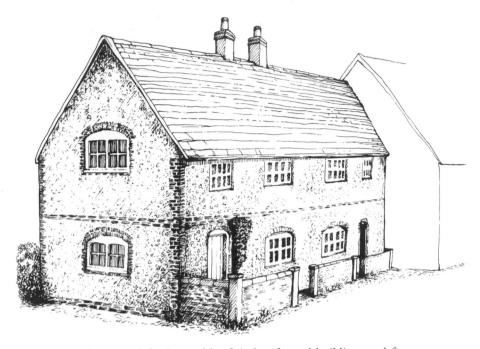

East Anglia is noted for its wealth of timber-framed buildings and fine parget-ting, but in the northern parts of Norfolk and Lincolnshire there is a traditional style of flint and brick construction. Like most regional variations of buildings, much depended on which materials were available locally to set the style.

shouldered 'Dutch gables' to be seen on many a 17th century brick house.

The timber tradition of Suffolk rapidly gives way to brick in the Fens, although few of the buildings there are very old since it was a sparsely populated area until it was fully drained in the 18th century. Among Peterborough's claims to fame is that the biggest brickworks in the country are to be found nearby.

In north Norfolk, too, few timber houses are to be seen because of the local scarcity of wood. Here the traditional walling material was flint, often simply laid roughly shaped and in irregular courses, but not infrequently neatly 'dressed' and, combined with bricks, worked into pleasing geometrical patterns. (Details of flint walling techniques on p 92.) Houses of cobbles and pebbles are also to be found, but few other stone-built houses are to be seen in the area, simply because it is not locally available. There are, however, a couple of exceptions: Stamford and Oakham are built almost entirely of stone, which occurs in rare outcrops nearby.

Another common walling technique in East Anglia is the use of clay lump or 'bats' – mixtures of clay and straw moulded into bricks and laid in courses, with damp clay used as mortar between them. As it is vulnerable to the weather, clay lump must be protected with a layer of plaster or roughcast, so it is often difficult to identify a clay lump house, or distinguish it from a rendered timber-frame one. It was also quite common, particularly when brick became widely available in the 19th century, for houses and cottages to be given an outer skin of brick.

The continental influences are to be seen in East Anglian roofs too, in the curved pantiles that are common in the area – both red in colour and, especially in Norfolk and Suffolk, glazed black. Such pantiled roofs are pleasing (and much more interesting that the flat, dull, blue-grey slates that were to replace them), but the real glory of East Anglian roofs is thatch. Few regions can boast so many surviving thatched houses, Suffolk being particularly well endowed. The best and most beautiful thatch is that of Norfolk reed, which gives a neat and tidy finish and lasts for generations (see thatching materials and techniques, page 72).

Central England

The central counties of England, stretching from Nottinghamshire in the north-east to Herefordshire in the south-west, have not in the past enjoyed so great a prosperity as their neighbours in the south-east or wool-boom East Anglia. So they have not seen so many houses of sufficient quality to withstand the passage of time. Nonetheless there are still some fine old houses and – in some areas, notably the Cotswolds and in Shropshire – there are delightful local styles found nowhere else. Only in the east and west Midlands, densely populated as a result of the Industrial Revolution, is the paucity of ancient houses really noticeable.

In the rural parts of central Britain, one very pleasing aspect is the preservation of older buildings in their original settings, stranded by the ebb of local prosperity. In rich times a village of fine houses could spring up, but as times again became hard, there would be little further development or even alteration. Many of the stone villages in the Cotswolds, for example, have been preserved by this process. It was not, however, necessarily a rapid affair. Although the uniformity of design in many a Cotswold village seems to imply that all the houses were built in the same period, the style varied very little for two or three centuries. Both prosperity and decline could have occurred over long periods. So a house with gabled dormers rising out of the front walls and with stone copings to the end windows – a typical Cotswold style – may have an Elizabethan look to it, but could well have been built in the 18th century.

The small towns and villages, built in the richly coloured local limestone blend perfectly and timelessly with their surroundings and the feeling of naturalness is frequently enhanced by the lichen covering the stone-tiled roofs. Prime examples (and there are many others) are Cirencester, Stow-on-the-Wold, Chipping Campden and Burford. At the other end of the limestone belt, which provided readily-available, easily-workable building stone, lie Northamptonshire and Lincolnshire, but here the stone looks much yellower. Towns built in it seem less natural than the Cotswold villages and buildings often look better cleaned rather than weathered.

In the central region, due to excellent local clays, brick making began early: from 1600 onwards bricks were used to build great mansions in the

The style of the stone Cotswold dormered cottage varied very little over two or three centuries. Sometimes they were thatched, but more often, as in this example, the houses were roofed with local stone tiles, giving a feeling of naturalness and harmony with its surroundings.

south Midlands. But timber was not forgotten and triumphs in timber-frame building are still to be found, notably in Shropshire, where a feature is heavy ornamentation and elaborate design. Architecturally the two most important towns in the area are Ludlow and Shrewsbury, each containing fine examples of flamboyant timber-frame building. The famous Feathers Hotel in Ludlow shows the style in its extreme, well over half the wall being covered in deeply-carved timber. Not quite so ornate, but still magnificently imposing, is Ireland's Mansions in Shrewsbury, a four-storeyed 16th century house with heavily-beamed bays and dormers.

In neighbouring Herefordshire, a characteristic is very heavy framing timbers, and the country also contains fine examples of late timber buildings, as do Worcestershire and Warwickshire, for here the timber tradition stood out longer against the change to brick. Dense forests and less demand for charcoal for iron-making than in the south-east seem to have kept the timber tradition alive longer.

59

Northern Region

The northernmost counties of england were originally very thinly populated and far fewer houses were built here before the 18th century than elsewhere in the country. Not until the Industrial Revolution was there any major expansion in population and building. The lack of forests in the north also means that timber houses are few, although there are a couple of notable exceptions: Chester and Cheshire and the City of York. York, as England's second city, had long commercial, political and ecclesiastical importance, and was full of timber-framed buildings. Many of these now hide behind Georgian brick facings, but others are relatively unaltered, as in The Shambles, a medieval street of overhanging jettied houses.

Cheshire is famous for its elaborate black and white timber houses, enhanced with curved wooden braces and diagonals across the whitewashed panels. Such magnificent 'magpie work' however, was usually confined to larger houses, of which Little Moreton Hall (1559) is the most famous example. Cheshire still also contains some fine examples of cruck houses (see page 13). It was a favourite style in timbered areas of the region even for bigger houses.

In Chester itself, the most striking timber buildings are The Rows, with continuous galleried walkways at first floor level. Originally houses of wealthy merchants, most of the surviving ones dates from the 15th and 16th centuries, although there was considerable Victorian replacement and renovation.

As one travels further north, however, timber houses become much scarcer, and stone takes over. Regional variations in design are determined more by the qualities of the stone and how easily it can be worked than by fashion. Because of the area's remoteness, change in style was a slow business anyway and often there was little variation for generations. Any changes that did occur, came much later than in the south so caution is needed when trying to date the stone houses of the north: they may well appear, stylistically, to be a century or so older than they actually are.

In the north-west of the area, sandstone dominates. Being relatively easy to work it allows building in well-fashioned blocks (called ashlar) or regular courses. Towards the Pennines, however, millstone grit, a much harder and more brittle stone, takes over – and here the houses tend to have rubble walls (mortared or sometimes even dry stone) with well-dressed blocks used only at the corners and around the doors and windows. On the north-east coastal plain, softer stone – limestone – reappears and with it houses in better fashioned blocks or stone courses.

The stone gives colour to the older buildings of the region: pinkish-reds in the sandstone area, the greys of the millstone grit which tend to blacken in the air, and the pale-grey limestones of Yorkshire and Durham. In the Lake District local slate was used, both for roofs and in dry-stone walling and locally-found volcanic stone – tuff – gives a pleasant greenish to look to houses in the area.

The oldest houses of the region are the longhouses, the traditional dwellings of the hill farmer and his family (and, initially at least, his animals). Built low and squat as protection against the weather, the longhouse has a shallow-pitched roof, covered with slates or more commonly, originally at least, with stone slabs. The chimney is squat too, and often with the windproofing cover of a pair of stone slabs or slates in the shape of an inverted 'V'. In many of the older houses the size of the stone blocks was massive in relation to the wall, giving a rather curious appearance but nonetheless great longevity and a capacity to withstand the roughest weather.

Stone buildings were common in Northern districts. Styles were very slow to change through the centuries up to the Industrial Revolution. The basis of these houses was the long house. Built low with a shallow pitched roof to withstand the weather, it was the traditional home of the hill farmer and his family.

In the 16th and 17th centuries farmhouses on the coastal plains, stone mullioned windows were a feature and are still to be seen, although unfortunately they are often eroded by polluted air.

In the counties abutting the Scottish borders – Cumberland and Northumberland – the longhouse gave way to the Tower House, a fortified bastion against border raiders and cattle reevers. Known as Bastel or Pele houses, these square or rectangular towers rose to two or three storeys. In the earlier ones, built from the 13th century onwards, living accommodation was on the first floor, with cattle beneath; while in later ones, built up to the 17th century, all the house was used for was human accommodation. Almost all the tower houses that survive have been altered or incorporated into larger houses. One interesting group are known as Vicar's Peles, because they were used as clergymen's houses. They were built near churches, which were also targets for cross-border raids and examples are to be found at Corbridge and at Alnham, Elsdon, Embleton, Ford and Whitton.

By the 17th century brick was to be seen increasingly everywhere and in both the east and west coastal plains there were good clays for brickmaking. Through the 17th and 18th centuries the local bricks were hand-made and fired in clamps, until machine-made bricks became available at the turn of the 19th century. To the east of the Pennines the demand for bricks grew more slowly than in the west, where industrial development rapidly brought in more labour and led to the building of vast numbers of houses in the characteristic vivid red bricks of the area, of which 'Accrington Bloods' are an example.

3

THE HOUSE
IN DETAIL

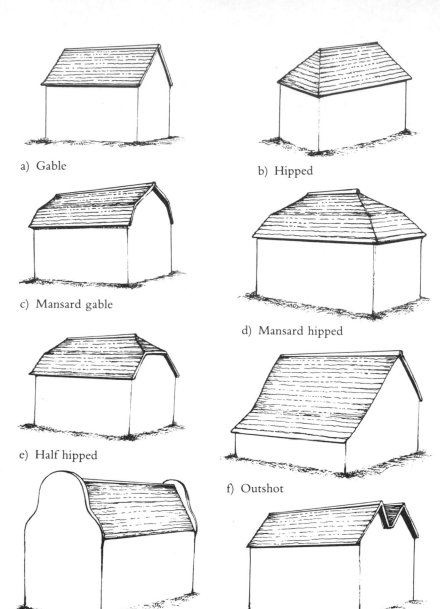

a) Gable

b) Hipped

c) Mansard gable

d) Mansard hipped

e) Half hipped

f) Outshot

g) Dutch raised gable

h) Double roof

The Roof

The roof is the most important structure in any house and also the most difficult to raise both safely and soundly. As well as combating the force of gravity, which wants to pull the construction tumbling downwards, the builder has to contend with outward pressures, which tend to make the roof splay. For the cathedral and church master builder, supporting his roof with pillars and soaring masonry arch, the buttress and the flying buttress were the solution to containing these outward thrusts. For the house builder the ultimate answer was to hold the roof together internally, with timber beams, rather than constraining it from outside. A variety of designs to do this evolved over the centuries but the basic techniques developed by the early carpenters can still be recognised in the construction of our roofs today.

EARLY ROOFS

The house of the English peasant, it seems, varied very little from early Saxon times right to the end of the Middle Ages. We lack precise details because the earliest timber houses still standing date from the 13th century, but from earlier remains, and from historical accounts, we can build up a picture of the very earliest dwellings.

There are two basic components to a roof: the raftering, or supporting structure, and the covering, generally known in early times as thatch, whatever the material used.

A rafter is simply a wooden pole and for most of Prehistoric Britain, thick with forest, poles of all shapes and sizes and suppleness were readily available.

As for the thatch, archaeologically, evidence of roof covering rarely survives, but turf, heather, bracken, reeds or straw could have been used depending on availability. Many Iron Age houses, whether stone or timber, oval or circular, had internal or external porches. The occurrence of the latter would have affected roofing.

The problem with a circular structure is that, unless the roof pitch is steep and the side walls of reasonable height, the usable vertical space is small compared with the horizontal area enclosed.

The Roman administration brought with it revolutionary techniques in town design and house construction. The Roman carpenter with his well-fashioned tools could construct strong rectangular frameworks for a variety of buildings in the newly founded towns and for the villas scattered around the countryside. These buildings frequently boasted clay tile or stone slate roofs.

At the end of the Roman period, however, as the administration and economic organisation broke down, the towns and villas fell into decay.

What emerges in the Saxon period are two styles – the sunken hut, and the hall. Sunken huts have floors sunk in the ground to a depth of up to three feet. Sometimes, as at Mucking in Essex, there is evidence that these sunken floors were the actual occupation level – giving maximum living space for the minimum building materials: the turves seem to have provided walling materials for the longer side walls, supporting rafters roofed with straw, bracken or turves. Sometimes, as at West Stow, the sunken area seems to have been an underfloor pit with the occupation floor at ground level above it. These sunken huts were frequently ancillary to a larger ground level building and it is this longhouse which formed the starting point for the medieval building tradition.

The grandest manifestation of this was the great hall. (For sectional drawing of the aisled hall house showing the roof construction see p8.) The roof rafters of square timbers were on an impressive scale, supported not only by the stout box frame or planking of the walls but also by an elaborate ancillary system of oak posts and beams which gave additional strength. The roof may have been 'hipped' – that is there were no high gable end walls but rather the thatch was carried round the ends on high rafters. Early halls appear to be almost all roof.

The basically triangular cross sectional structure was undoubtedly repeated in longhouses much smaller than the Hall where the building provided shelter for the animals as well as people. Examples are known where foundation trenches for the side walls are deeper than those for the end walls – presumably because the side walls took the main weight of the roof.

The Saxon roof covering continued to be turf, bracken, reed, straw or heather, or shingles – wooden tiles made from the off-cuts when the logs were squared.

THE CRUCK FRAME

The essentially triangular cross section had always created problems of head room in the smaller houses in relation to ground area covered. One solution that emerged was the cruck frame. By selecting for the major roof support timbers that were slightly curved or angled, the builder could convert the triangle into an arch. the best crucks (the word is a variation of crook) were made by sawing a curved beam in two down the middle so that the two halves could be pegged together at their apex to form a perfectly symmetrical support. The basic module consisted of two oak crucks, set some 16 feet apart, usually supporting a horizontal ridge piece. The crucks were strengthened with tie beams below the apex and joined with purlins.

The next step was to give even more internal headroom by extending the tie-beams so that they ended directly above the base of the crucks and then linking these ends with longitudinal members, which were known as wall-plates. Alternatively the vertical wall posts supporting the wall plate were pegged to the outside of the cruck and linked to it at wall-plate level by a short timber spur jointed to the cruck blade. Common rafters could then be run from ridge piece to wall-plate and the thatch now no longer reached so low. The walls were braced with vertical posts called studs and filled in with material like wattle and daub (of which more details in chapter on walls). Bigger houses could be built by simply adding extra similar bays.

Crucks were usually fashioned from oak, sometimes from chestnut. Together with the other, equally bulky, timbers for tie-beam, wall-plate, ridge-piece and the like, they were sawn and shaped in the carpenter's yard, and their joints cut out and marked up with code numbers ready for transport to the building site. Erecting the house was still very much a co-operative venture, with not only the owner's family joining in but other members of the community too, especially in the strenuous task of manhandling and levering the cumbersome crucks into position.

At first, it seems, crucks were erected without foundations, although the ends of the timbers were charred to try to help to preserve them. Later, ground sills were used and even dwarf walls of stone or brick, to give more height to the living space and reduce rising damp.

At the apex of the cruck there were various configurations. The two curved beams might meet and be jointed and pegged together, or they might even criss-cross each other, but a common design was to span a small gap at the top with a short saddle beam, on which the longitudinal ridge-piece of the roof would rest. For greater stability a collar beam was usually inserted a few feet from the apex.

There were many different arrangements, too, in the beams and timbers that helped to support the roof structures and delineate the walls. One important technique was to fix a tie-beam across the crucks, at the point where they began to curve, with its ends projecting. On these rested the wall-plates which in turn supported the feet of the rafters. Walls thus bore none of the pressures of the roof and could be built with wattle and daub panels or mud, although in some areas where it was readily available, stone was used too. Whatever the precise internal arrangements of the timbers, the basic arched shape of the construction gave much more headroom and at least those of more modest means – peasant farmers say – could live in something better than a cramped hut.

In the 16th and 17th centuries there were to be further changes in cruck design and construction. Several techniques evolved so that less wood, and shorter timbers, could be used. In one arrangement the cruck started near the ground but ended well below the ridge and was surmounted by a trussed roof. In another type, the arch was not formed from single timbers, but from two suitable shaped shorter lengths pegged together. (For an example of a cruck frame house see p 12.)

THE BOX FRAME

The alternative building system is the box frame (also known as the timber frame), and it is this form that predominates in the surviving earliest houses of the south and east. Again its precise origins are uncertain, but it was around before the Conquest: woven into the Bayeux Tapestry, for instance, are pictures of box frame houses being passed by the conquering army.

The basic box frame, as its name implies, is a construction of beams and posts jointed together to form a hollow box. The four corner posts, resting on ground-sills, are joined at their tops laterally by tie-beams and longitudinally by wall-plates. Again bigger houses or barns could be built by repeating the module as many times as necessary. The box has two distinct advantages over the cruck: it can support a higher roof and it can be extended sideways as well as lengthways. In mounting a roof on top of the frame, the builder had, of course, to find ways to counteract the ever-present tendency of his pairs of rafters to splay outwards. A heavy ridge beam (often, although not always, incorporated) added to the difficulties. Transverse collar-beams helped, and curved pieces called wind-braces were also added to give extra strength to the supporting structure where vertical corner posts joined the horizontal beams – and at other points where strengthening against the force of the wind was required. (For sectional drawing of box frame house showing the roof construction see p 15.)

ROOF TRUSSES

A better solution to the problems of splaying emerged with the evolution of the crown post roof. The crown post rested on a tie beam and supported another beam running centrally along the length of the roof space (the collar purlin) on which in turn rested collar beams joined to the rafters at each end. In this way much of the weight of the roof was supported on the tie beams. The crown post could be further strengthened by braces running to the tie beam, or to the collar beam and collar purlin, and often the posts were decoratively carved.

The medieval carpenter also developed ways of supporting his principal rafters without the need for obstructive tie-beams in the central roof-space. This he did by using curved timbers in arch or scissor configurations or, perhaps the most splendid of his innovations, in the hammer beam roof. Short beams (the hammers), supported by arched braces, project inwards, usually at wall-plate level, and support a superstructure of beams, struts and braces which takes the weight of the roof and counteracts the lateral thrusts. The hammer beam effectively narrows the span of the roof and distributes its pressures more evenly. It was only used, however, in the bigger houses and in grand halls, like the magnificent Westminster Hall, built for Richard II in the 1390s. Its roof spans 68 ft.

Many styles and systems of roof support developed, their structures due more to the inclination of the builder, the suitability of his timber and local tradition than to a truly scientific appreciation of all the thrusts and forces involved. Commonsense and experience were the rule of the day. Two basic designs won widespread acceptance however: the king-post roof and the queen-post roof.

Hammer beams were used to support the principal roof rafters without the need for tie beams. The short beams, plus the superstructure of beams, struts and braces, took the weight of the whole roof and distributed its pressure evenly.

The king-post runs vertically from tie-beam to ridge piece (or occasionally, from collar beam to ridge piece). Queen-posts are pairs of uprights placed symmetrically on the tie-beam (or collar beam), connecting it to the rafters above. Sloping struts connecting king or queen posts to the principal rafters give extra strength. These styles of roof supports, a frame of timbers joined together to bridge a gap, carry a weight and be self-supporting, are known as trusses. They formed the basis of almost all roofs right through to Victorian times; house styles varied considerably through the centuries but the supporting structures beneath changed little.

There was, however, in the 18th century, one development in the way the covering was fixed. The roof had no common rafters: instead thin wooden boards were fixed directly to the purlins, and then slates (usually) were nailed to the boards. Most modern roofs, however, have returned to older fixing methods, using battens nailed across rafters.

The development of the steam saw in the 18th century brought about much standardisation of roofs, for pre-cut truss beams and posts could now be turned out in large numbers. Some builders, such as Thomas Cubitt who built Mayfair, Belgravia and Pimlico, even had their own woodyards to produce the pre-fabricated pieces.

Although their essential structure altered little through the years, roofs can give us valuable clues about the date of the house beneath them: not in the covering, for that may have been changed many times, but in the principal timbers under it, for they are likely to be original. An old house with a steeply-pitched roof, for instance, was undoubtedly originally thatched with reed or straw, even if it is tiled or slated now. The amount of timber used can give a clue too. From the late 15th century onwards, as wood became increasingly scarce, less and less was used in truss constructions, so they became lighter and less ponderous. And while oak was used almost exclusively in the 13th, 14th and 15th centuries, other woods like elm and chestnut began to replace it from the 16th century onwards.

THE ROOF COVERING

Externally roofs come in a variety of shapes, and the roof of any old house is likely to have been altered and added to over the years. There are two basic styles: the gabled roof and the hipped roof. With the gable, the end walls extend vertically to the ridge, while in the hipped roof the vertical wall stops at the tie-beam and the end of the roof itself inclines inwards. The advantage of the hip is that there is less end wall exposed to

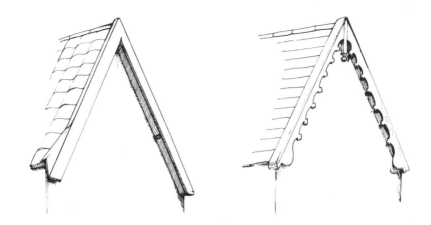

To protect the gable ends of houses which would be exposed to damage from wind and rain, barge boards were added. Early examples would be quite plain, but by the 19th century they would often be decoratively carved.

the elements; its disadvantage is that the roof structure becomes more complex and the space in the loft is lessened.

One solution to that problem is the mansard roof, first designed by the Frenchman Francois Mansard in the 17th century. Here the roof has two different pitches, the lower steeper and broader than the upper one. The mansard principle may be applied to both hipped and gabled roofs.

A great many roofs, however, are hybrids, like the hipped-gable (or half-hipped) roof, or the gable-hipped (or gambrel) roof. The word gambrel refers to the shape of a horse's hind leg and the small upper gable ends of these roofs, known as gablets, were originally left open or louvred to allow smoke to escape from the hall beneath.

Because of the problems of supporting a wide-span roof, early medieval houses tended to be narrow, just one room deep. The easiest way for their owners to extend them in depth was to add what amounted to a lean-to at the back, continuing the line of the original roof. Such 'outshot' roofs (sometimes called 'catslides' in the north) would often end only a couple of feet above the ground. Another alternative was to build what were effectively two narrow houses, one behind the other with the roofs taking the shape of an 'M'. One other roof style worthy of note is found mainly in East Anglia, where the steep pitch of the roof changes to a shallower one for just two or three feet above the eaves. The idea of this is to give the wall face a greater protection from the elements.

71

In gable-ended roofs, the horizontal beams of the supporting structure were often exposed to wind and rain. They were protected by timber bargeboards (or vergeboards), sometimes simple and unadorned but not infrequently carved with vigorous sweeping and interlacing designs. Another feature particular to East Anglian roofs is a thin cap fixed on top of the bargeboards, running back to overlap the first tier of tiles.

Thatch

Turves were the most important of the earliest roof coverings, although moss, bracken and heather were often used. Such roofs, however, would not last many years and they were gradually superseded by a far superior product: reed and straw thatch. Before the 17th century, most ordinary houses in the country were thatched and although many old houses were re-roofed with tiles or slates, particularly in the 18th and 19th centuries, there are still plenty left in country districts.

Reed obviously commended itself from the earliest times in those areas where it was readily accessible; and as agriculture got into full swing, increasing quantities of straw were available too. Thatch's advantages are its lightness, so it does not require massive roof supports, and its good heat insulation properties, conserving the indoor heat in winter and coolness in summer. Its drawback is the fire hazard.

The three most important thatching materials are Norfolk reed, combed wheat reed and long straw.

Norfolk reed, tough and durable, is the finest thatching material of all. The reeds flourished not only in the Broadland marshes but in the Suffolk and Essex estuaries (and Dorset ones too) and in other places with low-lying saltings. The light golden reeds, culled anything from 3 to 8 ft long, can be shaped into soft and undulating contours, the perfect complement to ancient walls and timbers.

Long straw is simply threshed corn, usually wheat, although barley and rye were used. For *combed wheat reed* the threshed straw is further 'processed' by removing the grain head and the outer leaves to reveal smooth reed-like straws. It was particularly popular in the south and south-east. Threshing machines ruined straw for thatching purposes and as R. W. Brunskill points out in *Vernacular Architecture*, 'there was presumably some relation between the spread of threshing machines in the north and west where other roofing materials were available, and their slow adoption in the east and south'.

Long-straw thatching uses cruder methods than those for the finer reeds, and it could often be carried out by agricultural workers them-

Before the 17th century most ordinary people's homes were thatched. Norfolk reed (as the example on the left) was considered to be both beautiful and long lasting, giving a neat and tidy finish which would last for generations. Long straw thatching (as the example on the right) used straw from corn threshed by hand. The introduction of threshing machines in the mid 19th century rendered the straw useless for thatching but recently farmers have adapted their methods to leave long straw once again available for the thatcher's art.

selves, who perfected their techniques by thatching haystacks against the winter weather. The wetted straw was gathered into rough oval bundles, some 16 to 18 inches wide and 4 to 6 inches thick, called yealms. These were laid on battens, starting at the eaves, and held in place by long strips of hazel, the sways, which were secured through to the rafters with iron thatching hooks. The yealms were built up in overlapping courses to the ridge, giving an overall thickness of some 12 to 15 inches.

The 'parting of the ways' at the ridge needed the extra protection of a cap made of several layers of straw bundles, again secured with hazel strips both longways and criss-crossed (liggers and crossrods). Extra liggers and crossrods were used, too, at eaves and gables. The finishing touch was to comb out or 'dress down' the unruly straw with a large wooden comb, called a side rake, and trim off with knife and shears the ragged eaves and barges.

The great advantage of reeds was that they had much greater longitudinal strength so each yealm could be 'dressed', that is, knocked into shape with the butt ends flush, as it was put up. This was done with a tool known as a leggett, a flat wooden hammer with bumps on it. Reed yealms could also be secured with sways and thatching hooks, but often skilled thatchers preferred tying them to the rafters, using a large needle to thread straw rope or tarred cords through into the roof space and back.

Reed roofs are more compact than straw-covered ones, with a much neater, close-cropped appearance. Liggers and crossrods were unnecessary at their eaves and barges. Norfolk reed, however, is not very pliable and so the ridge was capped with sedge, shaped, curved and decorated.

Thatched roofs require a steep pitch to carry rainwater safely away rather than absorbing it. Pitches vary from about 45° to 55°, or even steeper for long straw.

Reed roofs could last for a considerable time: Norfolk reed for as much as eighty to a hundred years and combed wheat reed up to sixty years. Long straw lasted less well – about twenty-five years – but had the advantage that it was much easier to replace.

Newer roofing materials like tile and slate at one time threatened the craft of thatching with extinction but it has now made a healthy revival.

Shingles

Another ancient roof covering was shingles, wooden tiles fashioned from oak and much favoured by the Saxons. They were used quite widely up to the 15th century, when the cost of timber began to price them out of the market, although shingled roofs as late as the 18th century can be found.

The average shingle was some 2 ft long and about 7 inches wide – and they were hung to overlap by about 8 inches. Their lower ends would be pointed and rounded (to pull water away from the joins) and also slightly thicker than the top. The shingle roof had a lifespan of some fifty to a hundred years, during which time the oak would weather to a beautiful silvery-grey. Like reed or straw thatch, however, their great disadvantage was that they were inflammable.

Stone

Stone, a strong, weatherproof and fireproof covering material, was used for roofs in those areas where workable stone for slabs was easily accessible. Sedimentary rocks like limestone and sandstone, which can be split along their layers, are needed and these are found mainly in the Pennines, and in the Midlands, the Cotswolds, Wales and the Weald.

Stone roofing material falls into two categories: thick, heavy stone flags, basically of sandstone and used chiefly in the Pennines, and thinner and lighter stone tiles, usually limestone, found particularly in the Cotswolds, South Wales and the Weald.

Flags can be up to 4 ft wide and 3 inches thick, and need a sturdy roof structure to support them. It is usually pitched at 30° or less, but even so the roof remains weather-proof because of the large overlap of each row. The lighter tiles were laid on a much steeper pitch – 50° or even more – and could be used on much more intricate roof shapes than the ponderous flags.

Both were fixed in basically the same way, being pegged into stout laths secured to the rafters. A hole was drilled near the top of the flag or tile and a peg of oak (or in the Lake District, sheep's bone) hammered home through it. The tops of the slabs were generally rounded or V-shaped, which helped to reduce the weight, but failure of the pegs was a common problem, as was erosion of the undersides of the slabs. Both flags and tiles were traditionally laid in graduated sizes, the largest at the eaves and the smallest at the ridge, although tile sizes vary less than flags.

To complete the waterproofing the stones were often bedded on moss and 'torched' on their undersides, that is, painted with a mixture of clay and hair.

In parts of the north it was common practice to use a combination of stone flag and pantile roof, laying three or four courses of heavy slabs near the eaves for solidity and protection against 'windlift' but covering the rest of the roof with lighter pantiles.

Tiles

Although the Romans were great tile makers, the tradition faltered, and reed or straw thatch continued to dominate roof coverings of most of England's houses until well into the 17th century. It was, of course, a great fire hazard in the towns. As early as 1212, for example, Londoners had been forbidden to roof their houses with 'Straw, Reeds, Rushes or Strubble'. Fired clay tiles, at first imports from the Low Countries, were available in the early 13th century, but they became increasingly expensive and hard to come by, because a great deal of scarce fuel had to be

a) Stone tiles were an early roofing material, most commonly in Kent and Sussex. They were nailed or pegged on battens and required heavy roof timbers to support their weight.

b) Fired clay tiles were first imported from the Low Countries as early as the 13th century, but only became a common roofing material when mass-produced tiles developed alongside brickmaking in the 17th century.

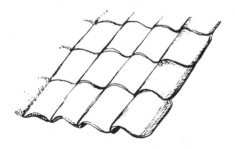

c) Clay pantiles began to appear in the 17th century, initially imported from Holland. They are most commonly found in eastern and north eastern countries.

d) With the development of canal and railway transport slate roofs became popular. Regular in shape, light and tough, a slate roof could last up to 100 years.

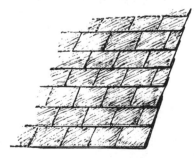

used in their manufacture. Not until new, more economic techniques were introduced in the 17th century could they really compete with thatch. These developments marched hand in hand with the advances in brickmaking, increasing numbers of tiles being turned out also by the expanding brickyards.

There are two basic types of tile: the plain, or flat tile and the curved pantile.

The plain tile's size – 10½ inches long by 6½ inches wide and half an inch thick – was standardised in 1479, but its early use, like that of bricks, was largely confined to the south, south-east and the Midlands, where slate or stone alternatives were not readily available. The plain tile is not actually flat but slightly curved, to help speed the water across its surface, and the old hand-made tiles with all their individual variations give ancient roofs a delightful undulating surface which roofs of mass-produced tiles entirely lack.

The tiles were hung on light battens, either nailed, or resting on their nibs, small clay bumps moulded onto their undersides. Each plain tile overlapped two others beneath it, so that only about 4 inches of the tiles' 10½ inches were exposed to the elements. Specially moulded tiles, to fit snugly into the 'valleys' of a roof and sweep round its hips, allowed quite complex roof structures to be covered. Half-round tiles capped the ridge and special bonnet tiles were also made for covering the hip corners.

Some tile-makers and house-builders enjoyed bringing bright patterns to their roofs with multi-coloured tiles, or picking out the date of building; and there were also more intricately-shaped tiles (fish-scales, for instance) which created pleasing patterns.

Pantiles are really a development of the interlocking Roman half-round tiles, but have almost a double roll to them, being in cross-section like a rather flattened S. They began to appear in the 17th century, as Dutch and Flemish imports, and their use tended to be confined to eastern and north-east counties, while plain tiles predominated in the Midlands and south. Local manufacture began early in the 18th century and a minimum size of 13½ inches by 9½ inches by half an inch thick was laid down by Act of Parliament.

The pantile only overlaps one tile beneath it, but its side-joints, the vulnerable part in plain-tiled roofs, are well-protected as the ends of the S overlap snugly together. Pantiles can be laid on a relatively low, lightly-timbered roof with a pitch of some 30° to 35°, while plain-tiles are usually hung on a steeper pitch, of 45° or more. Many pantiled roofs, however, have steep pitches too, for in areas like East Anglia they were often used as replacements for thatch.

When pantiles were hand-made, variations in shape made it necessary to lay them on a layer of reed or straw and hair mortar. Today it is common to use a couple of layers of bituminous felting beneath them, particularly on low pitch roofs. Because it is difficult to form pantiles around contours they are best used as coverings for simple roof shapes. Normally, of course, they are red-orange in colour, but an interesting development in East Anglia was the black-glazed pantile. The technique of dipping the tiles in a dark glaze probably originated in Holland but it became a speciality of Norfolk manufacturers in the 18th century.

Slates

Stone roofs, made of flags especially, had the disadvantage of great weight. Slate, found in north and west Wales, in the Lake District and Leicestershire and in Devon and Cornwall, can be split into much thinner slivers. It is, however, still a heavy material to cart around, so in all but the most expensive houses its use was confined to areas within easy reach of the quarries.

During the second half of the 18th century improvements in transport, notably the development of the canal system, gave slate more widespread popularity. Lake District slate especially was much in demand, particularly in the towns, as a substitute for inflammable thatch. (You can identify some houses that have had their thatch replaced by slate or tiles by the tell-tale marks the earlier, thicker, covering has left higher up the chimney stack.)

Welsh slate really became popular later, with the development of the railways and by the late 19th century it was in use everywhere. The thin blue-grey Welsh slates were riven (split) and cut into pieces of uniform sizes, each size having a colourful and feminine name; slaters dealt daily with, for example, 'large ladies', 'countesses' and 'queens'. These slates were laid in precise and regular courses. The slates from other areas, such as the Lake District, were thicker and less easy to work, so they came in much more random sizes and produced irregular courses. They were laid, like stone slabs, in diminishing sizes from eaves to ridge.

Slates were hung by nails on wood battens on low-pitched roofs (30° to 35°) and had a lifespan of about a hundred years: often the cause of failure is the metal nail; if this erodes the slate may slip, long before it is itself badly worn. Ridges were covered with hewn stone pieces, moulded lead or special interlocking slates called 'wrestlers'.

GUTTERING

It is necessary to keep the walls of a house as dry as possible to prevent internal damp and associated evils like mould and other fungal growths. The top of the walls, where the roof ends at the eaves, is especially vulnerable to the rainwater running down, and needs protection.

Thatched roofs present few problems because they are well over-hung and the water drips down a foot or more away from the walls. Early stone and slate roofs often had good over-hangs too, but a better way of ensuring that the water keeps away from the walls is to catch it in guttering, carry it downwards in a pipe and send it away from the house in a drain. Gutterings are also needed in the valleys of a roof, where two pitches meet at an angle, to speed water away from vulnerable joints, and around the border of a parapet roof.

Lead was an early material used, although because of the cost it was generally reserved for valleys and parapets. Cast iron and zinc were standard in the 18th and 19th centuries, although the iron tended to rust quickly and needed regular replacement. Today non-corroding plastics are the materials of choice.

REPAIRS AND RENOVATION

The main enemy of roofs, as of the house at large, is damp. It not only attacks the roof covering but in time can lead to a serious deterioration of the supporting timbers and could eventually cause the roof to collapse.

Thatch

While reed roofs should last a lifetime and more (up to a hundred years for Norfolk reed), their poor relation, long straw thatch, has a service life of only some twenty-five years. The signs of deterioration are easy enough to spot: the roof will look rather patchy and uneven, and moss patches will indicate areas of trouble. Perhaps the most conclusive of evidence is patches of damp in the (usually) plastered underside of the thatch.

Thatching is a skilled craft and repair or replacement is something best left to the experts.

A completely new covering, however, may not be needed, particularly if the thatch is of long straw. A fresh coat can simply be laid over the existing one, after it has been 'dressed down', that is combed out to remove debris, moss and loose straw.

It is generally recommended that with Norfolk reed the roof should be completely stripped, as encasing with an extra layer is often unsatisfactory. Combed wheat reed can be given a new coat, but again it is best to consult an expert thatcher on whether or not complete stripping is required.

The ridge capping in reed roofs is of a more pliable material – generally sedge – and tends to need more regular replacement.

Damage to a thatch roof from birds and vermin can be cut down considerably if the roof is covered with a stout galvanised wire mesh, although many purists feel that this detracts from its appearance.

Fire remains a hazard for the thatched home, a fact reflected in house-insurance premiums! The thatch can be fireproofed with a special solution but it is much easier to do this satisfactorily when completely re-roofing than to treat existing thatch. Even then the efficacy of the fire proofing can be eroded by the elements. New techniques, using fireproof blanket underlays, are being developed, and the local fire brigade may be able to advise on this.

Tiles, Slates and Stone

Slipped or missing tiles, slates or slabs are, of course the tell-tale signs of problems with these roofing materials and the cause of the trouble is usually the corrosion or perishing of the fixing pegs or nails, or by the failure of the battens onto which the covering is fastened. Frost and general erosion can also cause slates and tiles to split and crack.

The extent of renovation needed depends, of course, on the degree of deterioration, and on the aspirations – and solvency – of the householder. If the roof is not lined with felt it is probably a good idea to remove all the slates or tiles, fix a felt over the rafters and re-lay the roof. This will give both a second defence against water penetration and help conserve heat.

If felt is already fitted, or if the expense of removing the whole roof is not justified, then a patching operation can be carried out, removing the damaged or slipped tiles, slates or flags, making good the battens, and renailing or pegging the coverings. Tiles may be re-hung on oak pegs or with copper, aluminium alloy, or galvanised-iron nails.

All of the original tiles or slates that are still roof-worthy should be kept, and wherever possible, find similar old tiles or slates for the replacements. Nothing looks worse than an old roof patched with modern materials, and, indeed a modern roof (concrete tile, for example) on an old house leaves much to be desired. Original materials *are* scarce, but well worth searching for: the yards of demolition contractors are often a fruitful place to begin, or local farmers might be persuaded to part with tiles, slates or stone flags from tumbledown old barns or sheds.

When replacing a roof or a section of it, do not skimp with batten replacements: it is a false economy. Choose heavy gauge deal for preference and fix it to the roof timbers with copper nails (or if the ancient timbers will not accept them, with strong aluminium alloy ones).

Tiling and slating, like thatching, is a skilled job, and although the enterprising owner might like to do it himself he should take expert advice first, and may well find it is better to have a skilled craftsman to do the job.

Gutters

Faulty guttering is a common problem in the older house and can lead to damp penetration, particularly along the tops of walls. In many cases, however, the old gutter may not be leaking due to damage but be overflowing because of some blockage.

Cast iron and zinc guttering can be repaired with mastic materials although generally this proves to be a temporary 'patch up' solution. Replacements in metal may be difficult and plastic substitutes are often used. They can be disguised effectively by covering their grey finish with black paint.

Roof Supports

Once water has breached the outer defences and reached the roof supports, deterioration is not far away. Fungus infections soon bring rotting, and wood-devouring beetles thrive too in damp conditions. Signs of trouble are, from the outside, hollows in the pitched part of the roof and sagging or undulations along the ridge; and from within the roof-space, a musty smell, crumbling wood and the flight-holes of the beetles.

Early remedial action can be taken by the householder himself, but if major replacement of timbers (particularly structural ones) is required, or rampant rot or worms need eliminating, it really is best to call in the experts.

Both *wet rot* and *dry rot* are fungus infections. Dry rot is the most deadly, and unfortunately the commonest, cause of serious damage in old buildings.

Whatever the size of the timbers or quality of the wood, regular inspection and prompt remedial action will repay the effort. If the rot is affecting structural timbers, or if it is widespread, it is best to call in a local builder or a specialist firm.

Treatment should begin by eliminating the cause: repairing, for instance, the roof covering where the damp has penetrated. All affected timber should be cut away and renewed. In posts and beams, new wood may be spliced in, although badly-affected timbers should be completely replaced. It is always best to use well-seasoned woods of the same species for repairs and renovations: 'secondhand' oak from old barns or other buildings being demolished is usually to be found without too much difficulty in country districts. It should be carefully checked, though, to ensure that it is sound

After repairs, fungicide should be applied to remaining timbers, the new wood and brickwork, masonry and walling, to kill any residual spores and to prevent further attacks of rot.

'Wet rot' is an umbrella title applied to other fungi, which generally do not pose so great a problem since they cannot spread to sound timber. Wet rot may cause deep cracks along a timber's grain, but the 'cubing' effect of dry rot is seldom seen. Treatment is to cut away and replace affected timbers and spray with fungicide.

Beetle

Beetle infestation is generally described as 'woodworm', and that is fair enough, for the damage is caused by the larvae, or worms, of the beetle chewing their way through the wood. Although they make unsightly and rather worrying flight holes as they emerge, woodworm attack is rarely as serious as fungal decay.

Death-watch beetles have a preference for hardwoods, while the furniture beetle can be found in both hardwoods and softwoods; and can thus be a more serious pest in post-medieval houses, where sapwood began to replace the original oak.

You can detect which pest is enjoying your timbers if you spot one of the beetles: death-watch is bigger – 6 to 9 mm long, a browny colour with small patches of yellow hair; furniture is about 3 mm long, reddish to blackish brown, with short yellow hairs and lines along the wing cases. But since you are unlikely to encounter a beetle, the flight holes are probably your best clue. Infestation could have died out, or been eradicated years previously. The trick is to examine the bore holes carefully, looking for those that seem fresh and have traces of bore dust around them.

Woodworm can be effectively treated with a number of proprietary preparations specially formulated for the job which are sprayed into the timber. Treatment is best left to the experts and it is important to choose a firm which enjoys a good local, or even national, reputation. Timber which has been so badly affected as to have lost its strength should be replaced.

Whether the problem is beetle attack, fungus infection or a combination of the two, if the roof's structural timbers are weakened to the point where they are dangerously unstable, major repair work will be necessary. When joints have failed, major carpentry work is often required, although the judicious use of steel plates can sometimes provide a less expensive remedy.

If an ancient roof looks to be sagging or misshapen, however, it does not necessarily need instant repair, jacking up, insertion of steel plates or re-making of joints to stop the whole structure tumbling down. Oak takes a considerable time to season and the timbers matured after the house was built, altering their shape and shifting the structure. This is why many old houses look a little bent and buckled even though they are perfectly sound. The temptation to straighten them out should be resisted as this could actually cause serious damage to the structure.

The Walls

If the basic task of a roof is to keep out the rain, then the primary job for a wall is to keep the wind at bay. Many of the oldest houses did without walls, being virtually all roof. But gradually this was raised higher and higher and the wall came into being, low at first, but developing into a tall and rigid structure.

Some walls act as supports for the roof and so need strength to take its weight. Others are not load-bearing: if the roof structure is held up by a timber frame, the wall becomes mere in-filling and can be made of comparatively weak material, like wattle and daub.

The early housebuilders built their walls as their roofs, with materials that came easily to hand: turf and earth, mud and clay, rubble and stone. Only later, with improving transport and communication, did materials like brick come into widespread use.

TURF

The most primitive form of walling was turf. Close-cropped sods, anything from 2 to 6 inches thick, were cut and laid in courses like brickwork. At their base would be a plinth of rubble, and sometimes loose stones were placed on top as extra support for the roof timbers. Walls could be strengthened at their corners, or along their length, with wooden posts, but even so they were really no more than temporary structures.

CLAY OR MUD

Clay, or even wet mud, is much more durable. Many thousands of houses built of mud or clay several centuries ago in England are still standing. All a mud house requires, so the country saying goes, is 'a good hat and a good pair of boots' – the 'hat' being a thatch that keeps the rain off and projects it away from the vulnerable wall surface, and the 'boots' being dwarf walls of rubble beneath the mud to act as a surprisingly effective damp-proof course.

For proper protection, a mud-walled house also needs an 'overcoat' – a plaster or cement rendering – which can then be painted, tarred or whitewashed over. The overcoat often disguises the mud-walled house: the best clue to recognition is that it will often have rounded edges, both at the house corners and around the doors and windows. The internal rooms are generally small and the walls thick, several feet at the base and tapering gradually towards the top.

The mud was strengthened with all sorts of other materials: straw, animal dung, chalk and pebbles, for instance; if you were lucky, natural clays ideal for walling could be found locally. Whatever the materials, though, three well-defined techniques for using them grew up in different parts of the country. One uses a clay and straw mix laid in layers, the best known example being Devon cob. In the second, moulds or shuttering are filled up with earth or clay; and in the third, clay is moulded into blocks for laying like brickwork. These techniques were in use from medieval times right up to the 18th and 19th centuries.

Mixed Clay and Straw (Cob)

This was the commonest system and has been particularly used in the south-west (especially Devon), in the Midlands and in the north-west. It was also widespread in Wales, Ireland and Scotland. We will describe the Devon cob method, for the basic techniques are as used elsewhere, with a few local variations.

Loamy earth is the base material, mixed with water into a thick sticky paste. Added to it are a variety of strengtheners: chopped straw or reed, chalk, sand, gravel, small pebbles and stones. The glue-like mixture is then laid in layers, varying in thickness according to locality.

People in an area to the south-west of Aylesbury in Buckinghamshire were lucky in having a naturally-occurring chalky-clay which, when mixed with straw, proved an excellent walling material: called wychert, it is stronger than cob, so walls can be thinner. It is still to be found in many old houses in the area.

Earth Walls (Pise de Terre)

In this walling technique, loose earth was poured between timber or wattle shuttering and rammed in solidly: a more expensive and skilful process than the cob, it is much more common on the continent than in England. Not the least of the problems in our damp climate was finding suitable dry earth.

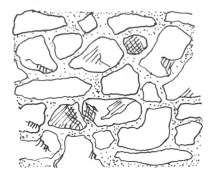

a) Random rubble

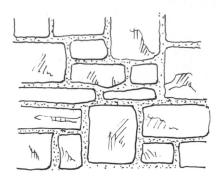

b) Coursed rubble

c) Granite and slate

d) Flint and brick

Clay Lumps or Bats

Clay and straw mixtures were also moulded in wooden frames into large oblong blocks, and allowed naturally to dry out (for up to a month) before being laid in courses like brickwork, with clay mortar between them. Such clay lumps or clay bats were generally confined to East Anglia, the technique having been imported from Germany or Scandinavia.

After being smoothed off, the walls were given a protective rendering of lime-plaster or primitive cement. Colour or whitewash completed them and was applied regularly giving the bright, tidy appearance so characteristic of many English villages with mud-walled houses and cottages.

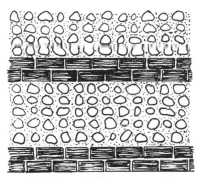

e) Pebble and brick

f) Chalk and sandstone

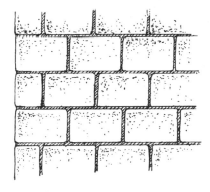

g) Ashlar stone

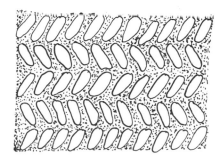

h) Diagonal cobbles

STONE

As a building material stone has an ancient pedigree. It was used in the earliest houses in the west and north of Britain where the scarcity of trees meant timber construction was not feasible. For their dome-shaped huts our ancestors picked stones from the ground, thus clearing their fields for tilling while providing material for shelter. Its capacity to stand the test of time also makes a stone a natural choice for monumental architecture, whether in the mysterious circles of Stonehenge, Avebury or elsewhere, or in temple and church, castle and cathedral. Stone buildings are generally only to be found where stone itself abounds. If an alternative is readily available, as timber is in the south-east and east, it will be used instead.

Britain is fortunate, however, in having a wide choice of stone suitable for building: granites and similar rock, sandstones and limestones, flints and cobbles. All such stones are used, and their different shapes, colours and textures give distinctive regional appearances to the older buildings of our towns and villages.

Geologists classify rocks according to their age and the manner in which they are formed. First, there are primary – or igneous – rocks 'from the fire', formed by the cooling and solidification of molten material from deep beneath the earth's surface. Granite is a prime example. Then there are the secondary – or sedimentary – rocks, made from the disintegrated fragments of other rocks, from dead and decayed organic material, or from chemical precipitation from watery solutions. They are formed in layers, usually originally beneath the sea, and among them are sandstones, limestones and chalk. A third type of rock is the metamorphic, formed by further action on igneous or sedimentary rock by heat or pressure or both. Slate is the most notable building material of this type.

Granites

Although in strictly geological terms, 'granite' refers to a well-defined type of rock, as far as the quarryman and the stonemason are concerned, it is a name to be used for a number of igneous rocks used as building stone. Igneous rock varies in colour and texture according to the conditions under which it was formed and what other minerals were amalgamated as the molten raw material (called magma) oozed beneath the earth. It solidified deep beneath the earth's surface but the subsequent weathering away of softer, overlying rock formations has brought it to the surface in many places.

Aberdeen, the granite city, is built of stone in which the crystals are all roughly of the same size, giving the buildings a grey, uniform appearance. English granites, such as those from Devon and Cornwall and from Westmorland, contain larger crystals of felspar, as well as those of the original magma, and so appear more interesting. Felspar can vary in colour from white to various shades of pink, and together with variations in other minerals trapped in the rock it contributes to many local differences in stone colour and texture.

One other igneous rock worth mentioning is tuff, a compacted volcanic ash. There is a deposit of it in the Lake District which gives a very pleasant greenish building stone often seen in the area.

Limestones

While the granites are found in the west – in Devon and Cornwall, Wales and north-west England – further to the east lies a long band of sedimentary rock also much used in building. This limestone belt stretches roughly north-east across the country from Avon and Dorset to the Lincolnshire and Yorkshire coast. Although less hard than granite, limestones are very good for building, being both durable and easier to work. Impurities in the rock mean that it comes in a variety of colours, from the famous mellow yellow of Cotswold stone to the creamy Bath stone of Wiltshire, the steel-grey Pennine limestone and the greyish-white or cream Portland stone (used in St Paul's Cathedral among many other famous buildings).

Sandstones

Sandstones are also sedimentary rocks, but softer than limestones and formed in a different way. They vary widely in texture from coarse to very fine.

Sandstone is found in various parts of the country, such as Sussex, South Wales, Shropshire and the north-east, but it is particularly prevalent in Derbyshire and West Yorkshire. The Millstone Grit of the South Pennines is perhaps the best-known, and is one of the strongest sandstones – but mention should also be made of the New Red sandstone of Cumbria. The Romans used it for constructing Hadrian's Wall, and many buildings in Carlisle and Penrith, for example, contain it.

York stone is a very hard and durable sandstone which from early times has found favour for flooring, notably in the Tower of London and other royal palaces.

'Marbles'

Metamorphic rocks – those that have undergone further changes due to heat or pressure, or a combination of both – include marble. True marbles, however, are rare in Britain and most so-called marbles are in fact very hard limestones. English 'marbles', which can be highly polished to resemble the 'real' thing, include Sussex marble and Purbeck marble.

Flints, Cobbles, Pebbles

Flints are irregular nodules of silica found in chalk. Although they are easy enough to dig out (the earliest mines were for flint) their irregular shape causes difficulties in building. they are used, however, in areas where other good walling material is scarce, such as in East Anglia, south and south-eastern England.

Cobbles are the rounded stones that can be picked from river beds or fields, while pebbles are smaller (80 mm across is usually taken as the dividing line) and generally found on the sea-shore. Cobbled walls are particularly to be found in Cumbria and Lancashire and in Humberside, while pebbles are prevalent along the East Anglian, Kent and Sussex coasts.

Building Techniques with Stone

Obviously the best way to build in stone is to cut the rock into uniformly-shaped rectangular blocks, to be laid in courses rather like bricks; such square-hewn stone is known as ashlar. It is of course the most expensive way and tended to be used for the finer houses with wealthy owners. The less well-off, however, could put on a show for the world: there are plenty of examples of everyday houses that are apparently of ashlar construction, but when you walk round the house you may find that the side walls are not nearly so well constructed, being made with rough masonry or of brick – and the back wall, hidden from public gaze, will probably be even more crudely put together. The beauty of the facade itself may be only skin deep, with a layer of ashlar backed with rough-hewn rubble masonry to give the wall its strength. In ordinary houses even the ashlar work was often irregular. Where the courses were of uniform depth, the length of the stones differed; more often than not the courses themselves varied in depth, diminishing towards the eaves. Ashlar, however, is distinguished in having a much smoother finish (dressing) than the hammer-rough blocks of irregular masonry.

Walls made of irregular stone blocks are the commonest in ordinary houses and it required great skills to assemble them into solid and satisfying constructions. The men inducted into these skills, the masons, guarded their methods closely, forming societies with strict rules of conduct.

There were two type of mason: the hewers or cutters of stone, and those who laid or set it in the wall, although often their tasks intermingled. In the earliest times convenient field stones would be used for walling, but these became increasingly scarce, and the Romans introduced quarrying and cutting techniques. Picks, bars and wedges were the tools of the trade, to split and prise away sections of rock, which were then sawn into blocks prior to final cutting and dressing.

The hewers of stone used mallet and chisel to shape their blocks. This was done at or near the quarry, for all stone is porous to water and when first taken it is wet with 'quarry sap' – a mixture of minerals and water – and most easily cut. Those who worked with 'freestone', that is limestones and finely-grained sandstones, became known as freemasons to distinguish them from the 'hard hewers' who worked tougher and more-difficult-to-shape stone.

When there is no timber frame in the building to bear the burden of the roof, the builder has to contend not only with the downward stresses but also with the forces that will tend to make the walls bow and buckle outwards. So load-bearing walls need strength at right-angles to the surface too, and in the house made of irregular masonry blocks this is usually achieved by making the walls thick and by placing in them frequent bonding or 'through' stones, running right back from the exterior to the interior surface.

The characteristics of the stone will determine the surface pattern of the wall, and this adds to the fascinating regional variations in the appearance of our houses. If the stones are very irregular, the wall may be jointed together in a number of ways. It can be laid without courses, that is with no obvious horizontal joints running along the whole length of the wall, or it may be 'built to courses', with stones selected and joined together so that horizontal strips of mortar are visible. Another alternative is 'snecking' in which there are horizontal joints but they do not run the whole length of the wall. Some local stone, however, like Millstone Grit, could be hewn into such regular blocks that the wall could be laid in courses with almost the same precision as bricks.

With the irregular masonry used in most stone houses, the largest and heaviest blocks were laid at the bottom of the wall (often large, rounded boulders were used) and the smaller pieces carefully selected and fitted together above them. Any large interior joints would be filled with loose pieces of waste stone, while the horizontal joints were originally packed with earth or clay, and later with lime mortar. Very irregular stones will require wide joints between them and for extra strength small stones were pushed into the mortar, a technique known as galletting. When the stone was particularly rough and of poor quality the wall would need re-inforcing with regular 'lacing' courses of better-quality stone or brick. Special attention, too, had to be paid to the corners, or quoins, which were built with superior-quality, better finished stones. It was common practice for the corners of a house, and the dressings around doors and windows, to be fitted by skilled craftsmen while the rest of the walling was left to the less-experienced men. The unit size of the stones used at quoins and window and door surrounds was larger than that of the rest of the wall, and where the wall was coursed, the courses aligned with those of the dressings.

Any opening in a wall detracts from its strength, so windows in particular tend to be both few and small in houses built of irregular stone pieces, but when good quality, well-cut stone was used skilled masons could produce a range of impressive, and beautiful windows.

Flints, cobbles and pebbles, because of their small size and rounded or irregular shape, presented particular problems for the wall builder. Masses of earth or clay, and later, lime mortar were needed to help with stability. Cobbles were often laid uncoursed while pebbles, smaller and of more uniform size, were usually laid in courses. In some areas naturally-occurring pebbles and cobbles were found that are flattened and elongated rather than rounded, and these could be laid in diagonal or herring-bone patterns.

Again, better quality material is needed around door and window openings and, although not absolutely necessary, it is often used at the corners too. In later houses brick was used, and it is found in strengthening lacing courses along the wall too. Brick is also often found in flint walls, both in lacing courses and interspersed with the stones to giving pleasing geometrical effects ('chequer boards' are common). Flints can be laid alone, either undressed, split or 'knapped', that is chipped to give a smooth and roughly square end, about 4 inches across. Rounded flints require plenty of mortar at the joints and often galletting for extra strength, while in knapped flint walls the joints are much thinner.

TIMBER FOR WALLS

Walls made mainly of clay, stone or brick can be described as 'mass walling', in that the weight of the roof and any inner floors is taken by the whole mass of the wall. The other technique is to build 'frame walls', where the load is taken by a framework of timbers and the wall itself is merely a non-load-bearing in-fill to keep out the wind and the rain. It may be that if timbers fail, or sag a little, the wall panels will bear some of the load, but that is not what they are designed to do. As described in detail in the chapter on roofs, timber frame houses are of two main types: cruck frames and box frames. The A-shaped crucks transmit the whole load of the roof the ground while in the box frame it is supported on a hollow cube of posts and beams. Between these two types are many hybrids, containing features of both.

Construction techniques varied, although both methods required the help of friends and neighbours to manoeuvre the heavy timbers into position. In cruck-frame houses, the crucks themselves were first pulled and levered upright and then ridge-piece, purlins and wall-plates were eased into pre-cut joints and sockets, to complete the rigid structure. Box frames, it seems, were usually built from the ground up: the vertical corner posts first being set in massive ground-sills or sole plates, then the longitudinal wall-plates and lateral tie beams set into joints at the top of the posts.

Timber houses were almost invariably 'built by numbers': the timbers were squared and jointed by the wrights in their own yards and taken by cart to the house site for erection. To make sure all the beams, posts and joists were assembled correctly, the joints were identified by chiselled Roman numerals, or by special gouged carpenters' marks, so that each tenon could be mated with its proper mortice. No nails were used in the construction, the whole frame being secure with wooden pegs, generally made of heart of oak.

From the earliest times, oak has been the timber of choice for houses, although other woods, such s elm, chestnut and willow, were used too, and with growing frequency as good timber became scarcer in the 16th and 17th centuries, partly because the best available oak was earmarked for the ships of the Royal Navy and much wood was used for charcoal burning. So the basic principle in dating a timber-frame house is: the more timber, the earlier the house.

Oak was used green and because of its tendency to warp, the early medieval builders used massive timbers to be on the safe side, a luxury the later builders were unable to afford.

The in-filling between the principal timbers of the frame varies in style around the country. In southern and eastern counties the space between the principals was filled with many vertical posts called studs. When timber was plentiful the studs often occupied as much space as the actual in-filling material, a style known as close studding, but as time went on the panels became larger and the number of studs was reduced.

In the western part of the country they preferred squarish panels, composed of both vertical and horizontal timbers. Again, as timber became scarcer, the panels increased in size. In some areas, notably Lancashire, Cheshire and North Midlands, the timbers, often highly decorated in intriguing patterns, were blackened with a protective coat of pitch in magnificent contrast to the whitewashed panels. This effect is known as magpie work. Elsewhere in the country the wood was left to weather naturally and the panels often colour washed, to give a more subtle but no less pleasing effect.

One curious feature of many 15th, 16th and 17th century timber houses is jettying, the upper floor overhanging the ground floor. Often

Elaborately patterned timber work, known as magpie work, was a common feature of timber-framed houses in the Midlands and particularly in the North West.

only the front wall of the house sticks out, although side walls could be jettied too. It has been suggested that building the upper wall further out produces a cantilever effect, to help stop the upper-storey floor from sagging, and jettying the upper storeys also gives further protection against the weather to the lower ones, but more likely it merely reflected a pleasing fashion. Jettying adds endearing dimension to many timber-framed houses, particularly as carpenters liked to show off their carving skills on the exposed joist ends and on the supporting corner timbers, called teasle-posts. When side walls were also jettied, the joists were jointed into dragon beams running diagonally across the upper floor. Where these beams jutted out from the corner posts there was further strengthening with brackets, again often pleasingly carved.

The most common way of filling in the panels between the timbers was with wattle and daub. The first step was to insert sprung vertical staves, fitted into auger holes in the lower side of the panel's top timber and into a slot in its lower timber, giving an effect like a barred window. Across these were woven supple withies, basket fashion, and on this wattle framework was then daubed a mixture of clay, dung and horse-hair, finished off with a coating of plaster, both inside and out.

Other in-filling included small stone slabs, wall-tiles and brick. When bricks are used the panels are often, although not always, whitewashed over. Such 'nogging' may be a later replacement for wattle-and-daub (in which case auger holes and slots may still be visible) or it might be original, for nogging is quite an ancient technique. The bricks were not only laid horizontally in standard bonds but vertically and in herringbone.

Cladding Timber Walls

The identification of timber-framed houses might seem to be simple, but although those with exposed timbers are indeed obvious at first sight, the majority of timber houses will not reveal their basic structure to the outside world: they were covered with a variety of claddings. This is particularly true of houses built of poorer-quality or second-hand wood. Not only did the covering enhance appearance, it also gave further protection against the weather and against the risk of fire. Walls might simply be rendered over with lime mortar and/or plaster or, from the late 18th century onwards, with cement. Or they could be weatherboarded, a technique much used in eastern and south-eastern England, and especially in Essex.

Clapboard or weatherboard was used on farm buildings from as early as the 16th century, and on timber-framed church towers from even earlier, but it did not really become popular for homes until the late 18th century and then generally only for smaller houses and cottages. Oak or elm were often used for the earliest weatherboards, pegged in horizontal strips to the internal timbers, but later deal, which was nailed to the studs, was the usual choice. The strips could be butted, but were more often overlapped and frequently rebated along the lower edge. Weather

The usual way of filling the panels between the timbers of a wall was with wattle and daub. Withies were woven basket fashion on vertical staves to make a frame. This was then daubed with a mixture of clay, dung and horsehair and finished off with a coat of plaster.

Weatherboarding in oak or elm was used as early as the 16th century, and most usually along the eatern coasts of Kent, Essex and Sussex. It served both to cover poor structural timbers and to protect the walls from exposure to rain and wind. It became fashionable in the 18th century, and was typically painted white.

boarding looks its best when painted white, although black and dark brown are other traditional colours.

Another cladding technique was to hang the wall with slates or tiles. In exposed areas especially, panels of wattle and daub were not really effective protectors against the weather, so when clay roofing tiles became more readily available and cheaper, they were quickly adapted for use on walls too. Laths were nailed across the internal timbers and the tiles hung on them triple-lap, that is with each tile overlapping two others below. Ordinary roof tiles were commonly used, with special moulded ones to cover jambs and corners, although very pleasant decorative effects were sometimes obtained by using different colours or tiles with shaped bottom edges, producing intricate geometrical patterns. When jettied houses were subsequently tile-covered, an outer brick wall

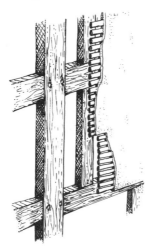

Plaster and lath could be used for both internal and external wall covering. Closely spaces laths, usually of split oak, were nailed to the timbers of the frame. Then this was covered with plaster made from lime and sand mixed with cleaned animal hair.

was often built around the lower portion of the house, in line with the wall above, to give a vertical face for tile-hanging.

Also used on walls were mathematical tiles, also known as brick tiles, for their purpose was to imitate the more expensive brick. Shaped to give an outward appearance of rectangular brick sections, or specially moulded for jambs and corners, these too were hung on laths nailed horizontally to the internal timbers. They were introduced around the middle of the 18th century and were much used in the south-east of England until well into the 19th. They were not affected by the Brick Taxes of 1784 to 1850, so town-dwellers particularly found that they could give their homes a fashionable brick-built appearance without going to the expense of the real thing. Further imitations of stone dressings at doors and windows, made from painted wood or plaster, added to the deception. Mathematical tiles were usually reddish-brown, but there are examples of yellows, greys and black.

Slates, cut small and nailed to laths, were also used in the south-west of England as a protective covering for timber-frame walls; and in the Lake District and North Wales, as an extra skin on stone walls, especially at exposed gable ends.

RENDERING

Rendering, the outer coat of plaster or cement, serves two purposes: it adds to the wall's weatherproofing properties and it can have a pleasing decorative effect as well. It is, of course, particularly suitable for walls of rough stone, but many timber-framed houses were also sheathed with an outer skin of plaster. The most popular early method was to mix clay with cow dung to make it more workable, and with animal hair for strength, and to spread the mixture evenly across the wall. In the west of England Wet Dash was a common alternative: a gooey mixture was literally thrown at the wall. Such rendering sticks better, but gives a rougher finish. Walls were then given a final coating of limewash (either white or coloured) which was renewed at regular intervals.

In the 13th century, plaster of paris was introduced and because of its brilliant whiteness it was used for a time as an external rendering. Its expense, however, meant that it was soon used only for interior walls.

Rendering really came into its own in the late 16th and 17th centuries with the use of lime plaster on a base of laths. It has been suggested that the technique became popular as a way of hiding away the scantiness of timbers by then being used in house-building. But plasterwork was used often in substantially-built early timber-frame houses, particularly in

East Anglia, and its main purpose must have weather-proofing rather than disguise.

The closely-spaced laths, usually of split oak, were nailed horizontally to the studs and other timbers in the frame and then covered with a couple of coats of plaster. This was made from lime and sand, mixed with fine cleaned horse or cow hair and beaten to a smooth consistency. The finishing touch was a coat of whitewash or colour wash. The eastern counties are especially rich in plastered and colour-washed houses and cottages which, under steeply-pitched thatched roofs, still grace many villages.

The plaster was not always left smooth: in many cases it had patterns inscribed on the surface, or was moulded into a variety of designs known collectively as pargetting (from the French *par* – all over; *jeter* – to throw). Such decorative mouldings were in use in the late 16th century but were at their most popular in the late 17th and early 18th centuries, again especially in the rich eastern counties. By the mid-18th century, however, fashion again favoured plain-plastered walls, both in new timber frame houses and in renovated old ones, although pargetting enjoyed something of a comeback in the late 19th century and elaborate plaster mouldings are still in use today. (For an example of a rendered pargetted house see p 24.)

The return to plain plastering coincided with the use of strong, smooth stucco as a rendering on buildings of stone or brick. The works of Palladio, the great Italian architect, were having a profound effect on British architecture in the 18th century. Not only were Palladian designs copied, but also the technique of putting a smooth rendering over all the rough stone and brick work, so that the eye can appreciate the building as a whole and not be distracted by joints and mortar. It is often difficult to distinguish houses built of stone and rubble and stuccoed over from those with timber-frames covered with lath and plaster. The best clues come at door and window openings, where the reveals in timber-framed constructions are generally narrower. In the 18th century, too, the quality of renderings was much improved with the introduction of cements which were both easier to work and gave a more durable finish. And the stucco was often incised with lines to imitate the ashlar masonry. (For an example of a Stuccoed Georgian house see p 34.)

Portland cement was introduced in 1824 and has remained to this day the basis for most renderings. Its greyish colour, however, is not particularly attractive and one way of disguising it was to pebble-dash the walls, throwing pebbles at the surface while the rendering was still wet. White cement, which helps overcome the problem, was not intro-

Above: Medieval pattern of moulded pargetting.

Left: Fan combed pargetting.

duced until the 1930s.

At first, stucco renderings were merely colour-washed but later were covered with oil-based paints which are more easily cleaned.

THE COLOUR OF THE WALLS

Through the centuries white has been by far the most popular colour for the walls of houses. It still is today: although a wide range of colours is now available, white still accounts for something like half of the sales exterior paints and finishes.

In times past almost every dwelling, from country cottage to castle keep, was painted white (like the White Tower, the initial building of the Tower of London, its white coating long since washed away). White helps houses stand out from the landscape and it is easy to manufacture: chalk dust or lime was the base, with some binding material, traditionally skimmed milk or tallow, to help stop the whitewash oozing away in heavy rain.

Such whitewashes, however, have only a limited lifespan and fresh coats need to be applied every year or two, although in time a good thick layer of protective lime can be built up. Modern cement-based paints give a much stronger and longer-lasting finish.

In the past, owners of more humble homes often did not bother to paint the whole of their house: perhaps only the front wall would be whitened or even just the surround to the door. Not everyone stuck to plain white: colours were introduced to make the more important houses and fortifications stand out from the crowd. And in some areas a strong tradition of colour-washed houses grew – Suffolk Pink being a case in point, for which bull's blood was added to the limewash. Soot and charcoal were other early colouring materials as was the root of the madder plant, or rose madder. Various minerals were also used: red cinnabar (mercuric sulphide), red and yellow ochres (ferric oxides), minium (red lead) and verdet (from verdigris, the green discolouring of copper). Later pigments used iron and manganese, and the brown earth, umber, which could be heated to give the deeper colour of burnt umber.

Complex and jealously-guarded formulae also gave medieval painters whites and yellows from lead-based pigments; vermilion from sulphur and quicksilver; blue from cobalt and a variety of other hues using, for instance, the oxides of antimony and tin. Medieval paints with metallic bases could be downright dangerous and colours were often unstable due to chemical interaction of pigments with the lime. This was not too much of a problem, however, because repainting was done so regularly. The 18th and 19th centuries saw the introduction of further colours – especially fresh blues, greens and yellows – and cheaper production of bright-coloured paints. Yet further pigments became available as a result of the revolution in applied organic chemistry in the late 19th and early 20th centuries, leading to a colour spectrum today of almost infinite variety.

When stucco became popular in the late 18th century it was usual either to mix-in pigments with the rendering, or to limewash it to imitate natural stone colours. But increasing air pollution in our towns led to a switch of oil-based paints which were easy to clean. Cream was a popular colour for stucco since it was nearest in colour to the fashionable Bath stone.

Oil paint had in fact been known as early as the 13th century but because of its expense, was seldom used for house exteriors. When high quality wood, notably fine oak, was used for house-building there was no need to protect it, nor disguise it with paint, although a covering of varnish and oil was often applied to doors to protect against scuffing and marking. With the introduction of cheaper woods, protection and disguise were necessary and white lead-based paints were commonly used, as other shades tended rapidly to discolour and fade. By the late 18th century a variety of longer-lasting oil paints for woodwork were introduced and often houses were painted in soft and subtle shades. But again the pollution of the air by industry forced the 19th century householder to search for more practical colours and black and ochre were popular early in the century, with chocolate browns (especially for windows) and dark greens and blues coming into vogue a little later.

Today's paints, in their wide range of colours, are mixed with a variety of modern materials such as polyurethane, for a tough and lasting finish. For rendered masonry and brick walls, coloured cements and cement-based and textured resin-based paints have largely replaced the traditional lime washes.

It is pleasing to revive and retain local colours and if you want to check on your local traditions the council planning or architect's office should be able to help. Black and white contrasts find particular favour in western districts; cottages and farms with white walls and black-painted quoins, windows and doors are common. It is interesting to note that while in Essex and Hertfordshire weatherboarded houses were usually painted black (they were originally tarred), in Kent, white is the traditional weatherboard colour. In other areas, notably East Anglia, strong colours like pinks and reds are often favoured.

BRICK FOR WALLS

Shaped, baked clay bricks have been used for building walls since the earliest times but they did not become popular for ordinary English houses until the 15th century, and it was not until well into the 19th that they were a universal building material. The Romans brought a superior skill in brick-making to Britain, but even so, it is rare to find Roman houses built solely of brick. Brick bonding courses, arches, floor supporting pillars are more common. Roman bricks were in general thin and perhaps the description 'wall tile' is more suitable than 'brick'. When the Roman occupation ended, however, the craft of brick-making was neglected, although the bricks themselves were highly prized and Roman buildings were plundered for them to use in new buildings, particularly to strengthen corners.

Bricks made something of a comeback following the Norman conquest, but again were mainly used for military buildings and in the fortified castles and keeps of the rich and powerful. The Normans at first imported large quantities of brick from the continent but later the home industry revived, the first English bricks being manufactured around 1200. Unlike Roman wall-tiles, these bricks were not cut to shape, but moulded, to a size some 1¾ to 2¾ inches thick and 12 by 6 inches across. Known as 'great bricks' they were made by hand and were often irregular, both in size and shape – and again were seldom used in ordinary homes, not least because of their expense. In the 13th century

Flemish craftsmen began to settle in East Anglia and soon introduced their brickmaking techniques there. Flemish bricks were somewhat smaller than the great bricks – some 8 to 9½ inches long, 3¾ to 4¾ inches wide, and ranging in depth from 1¾ to 2½ inches. Because they could be held more easily in a man's hand, they could be laid more speedily.

Bricks coming from any particular mould should have been of fairly uniform size but there were in fact quite considerable variations due to the temptation not to fill the mould right to the top. This was because bricks were sold in those days by number, rather than by weight, so there was more profit to be made by using less clay. To discourage such practices the size of bricks was regulated by law in 1571, the so-called 'statute brick' being of the harmonious proportions of 9 inches by 4½ inches and 2¼ inches deep.

In the 16th and 17th centuries, with England's increasing mercantile prosperity, there was a great rebuilding and, encouraged by increasing scarcity of timber, building with bricks became increasingly popular and widespread. By the end of the 17th century, they had become fashionable for public buildings (Wren's royal Hospital in Chelsea is a fine example), and the fashion spread to humbler dwellings. Not only were new houses constructed of bricks, but older timber-frame houses, for instance, might be completely encased in a new skin of brickwork, or a false front wall might be built of bricks. And brick nogging was increasingly used to replace wattle and daub as an in-filling between wooden frames.

Brick building continued to increase in popularity despite the imposition of a series of brick taxes between 1784 and 1850. The earliest of these taxed bricks by number than than size, which encouraged a temporary increase in brick dimensions. Even though length and breadth were fairly well standardised, heights grew – to as much as 3¼ inches. (Incidentally, bricks in the North of England are still traditionally somewhat larger than those in the South). The brick taxes, however, did encourage a revival in the building of timber-framed weatherboarded houses and in the use of imitation brick mathematical tiles.

Although increasing quantities of bricks were being made from the 13th century onwards, their early use for everyday houses was confined almost exclusively to the areas where suitable clays were readily available; as with stone, long-distance transportation was impractical before the advent of the canals and the railways. Half of the houses built in brick between the 13th century and the late 17th are in East Anglia, where a familiarity with continental techniques and local shortage of stone also helped to maintain brick's popularity.

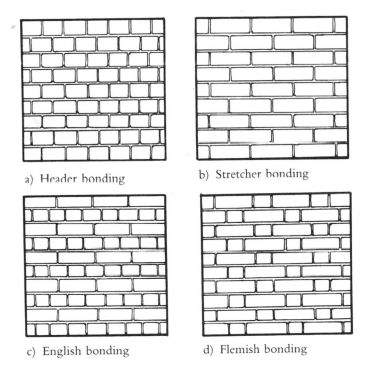

a) Header bonding

b) Stretcher bonding

c) English bonding

d) Flemish bonding

The early brickmakers were itinerant craftsmen, moving from place to place making and laying their bricks: they were skilled in both arts. Near many villages a brickfield may still be found, usually now an area of bumpy ground from which clays had been dug out. And by many a country house or farm you'll find the pond that was originally a clay pit. Bricks were fired in clamps on site – and those at the centre had the best firing. They were used as facing bricks while less well-baked ones were built into interior walls.

By the end of the 17th century good-quality brick-making was helped by the invention of the pugmill which mixed clays to an even consistency. By the time the brick taxes were abolished, in the 19th century, brick-making had advanced from a craft to very big business, using all the mass-production techniques brought in by the Industrial Revolution.

Bricklaying styles and colours

The earliest bricks were of irregular shape and size and although laid in courses showed no regular pattern or 'bond'. Later, however, a number of distinct styles emerged. In English Bond, for instance, there are alternate courses of *headers* (bricks laid so that their head, or end, shows) and *stretchers* (laid longways on). In Flemish Bond, introduced in the 17th century, there were alternate headers and stretchers in each course. There were many variations of these basic bonds, among them English Garden-wall Bond, where three or five courses of stretchers alternated with one course of headers; and Flemish Garden-wall Bond, where there were three stretchers to each header in every course. Other bonds, with their individual patterns, include Monk Bond, Rat-trap Bond, English Cross Bond and Header Bond, where each course is composed solely of headers, an arrangement favoured for decorative work. Today the most common arrangement is Stretcher Bond, every course consisting only stretchers. This is because of the widespread use of cavity walling, in which there are two separate 'skins' of wall, each of only a single brick's thickness. This method was introduced at the beginning of the 19th century.

Although most bricks have always been some shade of red, variations in the composition of clays from one locality to another has led to some striking colour differences, a variety further enhanced by the techniques of firing and the use of additives, like sand. Basically it is iron that gives bricks their red colour, and in Lancashire where the clay has a high iron content they can be almost scarlet in appearance. But if the iron-bearing clays are fired to very high temperatures, they can turn blue, as in Staffordshire bricks. Other notable regional variations, due to the presence of different minerals in the clay, include blacks, from Surrey, Sussex, Berkshire and South Wales; brown from Humberside; greys from Oxfordshire, Berkshire and Hampshire, yellows from the Thames Valley, and whites in Sussex and East Anglia.

Individual variations in any batch of bricks meant that old walls have marvellously subtle shadings of colour, but the bricklayer was able also to exploit more marked colour differences by laying bricks in decorative

This type of herringbone decorative brickwork was often used as an infill between timber panels, known as nogging.

Decorative geometric patterns of different coloured bricks were first used in late medieval and Tudor times. With later advances in technology and mass produced bricks it really found favour in Victorian house building.

geometric patterns. Some bricks for this were produced in special firings: a vitrified metallic purple was a popular choice. Decorative brickwork was much favoured in the Middle Ages and under the Tudors, but later, when stucco became fashionable, the craft was neglected. It enjoyed a brief reflowering, however, in Victorian times when new technologies produced bricks in a wide range of colours and a variety of finishes, particularly vitreous glazes. Further decorative effects could be achieved by using moulded, carved and rubbed bricks, both to produce imitations of classical forms and in marvellously intricate designs formed in the easily-workable brick. Terracotta, a refined material for bricks, was particularly suitable for mouldings. Although it had been introduced in the early 16th century its use was short-lived until a revival in the 18th, and again in the late 19th century. A splendid example of a public building in terracotta is London's Natural History Museum.

Even when brick was not used for whole walls, it found favour for dressings of quoins, window and door surrounds, while the rest of the wall might be, for instance, in irregular rubble masonry. Conversely, in areas where there was a strong tradition of stone-building, bricks might be used for general walling while quoins, windows and doors were dressed with good masonry blocks. And many houses that were built of timber, and even of stone, would have brick chimneys, because of the ease of building and brick's fire-resistant properties.

INTERIOR WALLS

Inside the house the walls have been given a variety of treatments over the years, ranging from the plain and simple of earlier ordinary homes to the elegant and fancy of Georgian and Victorian mansions.

In early timber-frame houses, when good oak was in plentiful supply, the wall beams and studs were left exposed, with the space between them

Wood panelling provided warmth and insulation to a room, while protecting the plaster walls from damage. It was prevalent in Tudor and Jacobean times, but fell from favour with the introduction of wallpaper in the mid 18th century. The example here shows a particularly finely carved Tudor oak 'linen' design with the edges carved to simulate stitching.

filled with wattle and daub, plastered over and coated with a limewash which was usually white but could be coloured. When wood became more scarce in the 17th century, rougher, cheaper and often secondhand timber was used and in this case the wall would be completely plastered over. This too was the normal procedure with mass walls of stone, cob, clay lump or brick.

In Tudor, Elizabethan and Jacobean times, particularly in the larger and finer houses, wood panelling was often fixed to the walls, not only to produce a mellow and elegant interior, but to provide insulation as well. The panelling, often finely carved, might extend to the full height of the room, or be perhaps just waist high. This lower half of the wall is known as the dado and its panelling was protected from damage by the backs of chairs – which were replacing stools and benches – by a protruding chair-rail.

Panelling, particularly half-panelling, was still popular in the early Georgian period but fell from fashion in the mid-18th century when wallpaper became the vogue.

REPAIRS AND RENOVATIONS

The ivy-covered wall has long been regarded as a traditional feature of older properties. Charming it may be, but it does the wall little good, pulling away at mortar between the joints, and its roots weakening the foundations.

Ivy is, however, a relatively minor problem for walls. Others with far more potentially serious effects include settlement, deterioration of wall fabric, penetrating damp and rising damp.

Settlement

Settlement is the result of the ground having given way or subsided beneath the wall so the foundation is no longer sufficiently firm. The collapse of old mine workings, the diversion of a spring or underground stream and even the ever-probing roots of adjacent trees, however, can cause settlement in a wall that has otherwise been standing safely for centuries.

It is difficult to cure and its diagnosis and treatment are best left to experts. Shoring and jacking up of the wall, and the roof above it, are normally required so that the foundations can be dug out and new, larger ones of reinforced concrete laid to spread the load of the wall over a greater area and so relieve some of the pressure on the ground. Brick and stone walling is unable to take tension loads (that is, to hang from above), so often the whole wall has to be taken down to prevent haphazard collapse, and then be rebuilt with the original stones or bricks, supplemented by extra material of similar size, shape and colour.

Deterioration of the Wall Fabric

The wall's basic task is to keep out the weather, and it is the weather that is the wall's greatest enemy. Different types of walling, however, fail in rather different ways:

Clay wall problems: to maintain their solidity and coherence, clay walls must be kept dry; so their 'boots', the damp-resisting base on which they are raised, must continue to be effective and the 'overcoat' of rendering has to remain substantially impermeable. Excessive damp in the wall causes a loss of strength which leads to an outward swelling, or bowing, of the wall, usually near its base. Once the swelling begins, all too often a vicious circle of degeneration begins, for since the rendering is more brittle than the body of the wall it will crack, letting in more water to increase the damage still further.

If the damp is rising from the ground beneath, the resistance of the base can be enhanced by adding or replacing a damp proof course. If the damp is penetrating from the outside because the rendering has deteriorated, it is often best to strip off the overcoat and renew it. In old rendered walls, patching of large defective areas is seldom a satisfactory solution for, whatever care is taken, matching for colour and texture is difficult, and anyway the fresh rendering will always weather differently. Small areas of patching, within definite lines such as at corners, can be successful, however, as the angles of the building will help to mask them.

Timber wall problems: although timber itself is not greatly weakened merely by being damp, the evils of wet and dry rot flourish in damp conditions (see chapter on Roofs for details) and prompt remedial treatment is recommended.

To protect the timber frame the insertion of a damp proof course in the supporting dwarf wall or plinth may be necessary, and rendering or infilling should be treated as described for clay walls above. When replacing rendering over a timber frame, extra protection can be provided by nailing a layer of roofing felt to the frame and then fixing over this a further layer of expanded metal mesh to act as the key for bonding the rendering to the wall.

A particularly weak spot in timber walls is the sole plate and rot fostered by rising damp can often cause perishing, occasionally dramatic enough to require replacement of the plate. So long as the rest of the frame structure remains sound – and, surprisingly, it usually does – replacement is not too difficult. The preferred treatment is to replace it with a similar baulk of aged timber, tenoned on to the existing studs to form an exact replica of the original. If the bottoms of the studs have also perished their ends should be cut back to sound wood and morticed into an elevated sole-plate, supported on a dwarf wall. A third alternative, far less costly, is to replace the sole-plate by brick or concrete.

Where the panels between the studs are of wattle and daub, these may have deteriorated in the course of time and become unstable. If they are merely loose, they can be refixed to the timbers by nailing, and then plastered over in the usual way. If there is severe deterioration, however, the panels are best removed completely and the space refilled. Breeze blocks are commonly used and when plastered over produce a panel virtually indistinguishable from the original.

Brick and stone wall problems: the commonest first form of deterioration in brick and stone walls comes from rain and airborne pollutants ravaging the mortar holding the units together. This is further aggravated by frost damage. The effect on brick or stone walls is to drive the individual blocks apart or, in extreme cases, to crack the bricks and stones themselves. Re-pointing, the scraping out of old mortar and replacing it with new, should be done fairly regularly to preserve old walls. There is a need for considerable care, and proper re-pointing can be both time-consuming and expensive.

The important thing is keeping the mortar softer and more porous than the bricks themselves. Old brickwork can be ruined by re-pointing with hard and impervious cement mortars.

If deterioration of the joints has been allowed to progress too far, the loads and pressures on it and within it can cause bulging, leaning and long ragged cracks. Here it is best to seek expert advice on the severity of the problem. Some cracks may have been caused by past settlement and the wall may now be stable; on the other hand deterioration may be accelerating, and prompt action needed to prevent a major catastrophe.

Whenever rebuilding is needed, as much of the original material as possible should be kept for re-use. It is often possible to track down old bricks from demolished buildings as replacements.

Penetrating Damp

Penetrating damp is an annoying defect in walls old and new not only through causing unsightly patches inside the house, fostering mould and discolouring decorations, but also in promoting conditions for the growth of structurally-damaged rot. Driving rain is the chief culprit, seeping its way through the walls, but leaking or overflowing guttering and waste pipes can cause problems too, and these should be regularly checked, cleaned out or replaced. Cast-iron 'rainwater furniture' often rusts due to infrequent painting, so regular maintenance with bituminous or similar protective paints is essential. The outside rendering should be checked regularly for cracks and bulging, and repaired or replaced as necessary. If damp still persists internally it can be treated with a number of proprietary waterproofing products available at builder's merchants.

Rising Damp

Rising damp is moisture conveyed by capillary action up a wall from the earth below. Modern houses have a damp-proof course (DPC) of waterproof plastic or rubber sheeting incorporated between a course of bricks just above the ground, but older ones do not. It is generally wise to install one to keep the damp down, for its effects should not be underestimated: rot affects not only structural timbers but joinery like skirting boards and door frames as well.

It is easy enough to build in a damp-proof course while constructing a wall but rather more difficult to install one in an existing wall. A variety of techniques are used, notably injection, where holes are drilled into the wall at intervals of about a foot, and a rubber or plastic solution pumped in under high pressure to form a waterproof 'course'. Another method is to insert porous tubes into holes drilled into the base of the wall, which are supposed to draw out the water rather like a land drain. A more time-consuming method damp-proofing is to dismantle the base of the wall, one small section at a time, and re-build onto it a layer of waterproof felting, or even slates. Although it does take time and cost money, it has proved very effective.

Internal Walls

Internal walls from the late 16th century onwards were often covered with plaster, laid on laths attached to battens. These unfortunately often require attention due to failure of the fixing nails or the depredations of rot and woodworm. Sometimes the loss of battens may be immaterial, as in the centre of mouldings and covings, for they were no longer needed for support once the plaster had set. When battens in long flat areas are lost or damaged, however, there may be sagging, bowing and crumbling of the plaster. Wholesale replacement of the batten and lath base with plasterboard panels if often not necessary, for weak areas can be strengthened in a variety of ways, using counter-sunk brass cups and screws for instance. Batten channels can be dug away to provide a key for a fresh coat of plaster, reinforced by a hessian or metal mesh backing. Keying of the fresh 'coat' is of prime importance and additional background for the new plaster to adhere to can be provided by 'switches' of metal threads hung from nails on the wall.

Replacement by plasterboard and replastering of flat areas can be done by the amateur handyman, but more sophisticated plaster renovation and repair is usually best left to the professionals.

Windows

Windows are among the most important feature of a house, adding much to its character. They are its 'eyes'; without windows the walls are blank and blind.

The well-lit and well-ventilated houses of today with their large glazed windows are vastly different from earlier homes. The earliest houses often had no windows at all, such light and air as did penetrate their gloomy and smoke-filled interiors coming from the single door opening. Even when windows were introduced, they were small and draughty affairs, their main job being to ventilate rather than to let in light. The word window comes from the old Norse *windauga* or 'wind-eye', although the Saxons used to call them *windi-durs* or 'wind-doors'.

As well as letting out some of the smoke these narrow holes let in the chill and damp, so they would be covered at night with wooden shutters or with animal skins, to give some protection as the fire burned low. To keep out birds and other intruders, a criss-cross lattice of withies would be built across them, or vertical bars, called mullions, fitted in.

Although the Romans were able to make glass – and did so in Britain – its use in the ordinary post Roman house is a comparatively modern luxury; glazed windows were used in many buildings by the third century AD, and fragments of window glass are found on many domestic sites of that date. In the post Roman period glazed windows in ordinary houses were uncommon until the 17th century and not widespread until the 19th century. Before that the owner of a small house or cottage had to be content with cheaper alternatives like oiled paper or fabric, or even the stretched placenta of cattle or horses: a mare's placenta was much prized as a window-covering by the Irish since it was said to be dagger-proof. The King's excise, too, with heavy taxes and duties on windows and on glass, robbed the common man for many years of the light and ventilation he deserved.

GLASS MAKING FOR WINDOWS

There was no glass-making industry in Britain for many centuries after the Romans left. Such glass as was used, in churches and for some of the more important secular buildings, was imported from the continent. The Normans, for instance, brought their glass across from France, and also imported it from Flanders and Germany.

Glass-making started up again here at the beginning of the 13th century, in a small way in a handful of areas which had suitable sands: in Surrey, for instance, and in Shropshire and Cheshire. By Tudor times, the larger houses were usually glazed, especially the timber framed ones, but glass windows were so highly prized that a house owner would often take them with him when he moved and it was not uncommon for windows to be bequeathed in wills. A law of 1579, however, decreed that glass fixed in windows could not be taken away, 'for without glass is no perfect house'.

Although the Romans had perfected techniques for making reasonably large sheets of window glass, most medieval glass came in small pieces of varying thickness which were jointed together with a lattice of lead strips.

The commonest technique for making glass was the crown or Normandy method. After a thick glass 'balloon' had been blown, an iron rod or 'punty' was stuck to it opposite the blow-pipe. Then the blow-pipe, together with an area of glass around it, was removed and the resultant thick vase of glass reheated and spun very rapidly on the punty to provide a flattish disc. The punty was broken away leaving a crown or 'bullion' in the centre. The circular sheet was then cut into square or diamond shaped pieces, called 'quarries', with an average size of about 12 square inches (75 square cm). Panes of crown glass are easily recognised by the curving sweep of the air bubbles trapped within them. Incidentally the bullion, or bull's eye, now so eagerly sought after as antique 'bottle glass', was regarded as inferior and it was used only in less important windows or in shop-fronts. The lead strips into which the glass panes were set are known as cames or calms and their diagonal or rectangular latticing reflected the earlier patterns of withies used in unglazed windows. There are practical aspects to the use of a diamond pattern: the rain water runs more easily off the canes and you can cut more diamond-shaped panes than square ones from a disc of crown glass.

Another, but far less common, technique was to produce brodeglas or broad glass. A long cylinder was blown, its ends removed and a cut made along its length so the cylinder could be flattened out into a rectangular sheet.

Towards the end of the 17th century, major changes in architectural fashion led to the increasing popularity of the sash window. This meant a switch from leaded lights to wooden glazing bars, more able to take the strain of opening and closing. Larger panes of glass were also becoming available, imported at first from France, but later made in England, notably in the Newcastle area, and by the middle of the 18th century even small houses had sash windows. As the style progressed, and became more and more refined, the wooden glazing bars became thinner and thinner and by the early 19th century they were sometimes replaced by narrow strips of iron supporting the glass.

The use of glass, however, was sharply constrained in poorer dwellings by a series of Government taxes and excise levies. The levy on glass itself was first imposed in 1695 and it continued with the occasional let up for 150 years. In the early 1800s it could amount to as much as twice the actual production cost of the glass itself. Even more damaging to the development of light and airy houses was the notorious window tax, also introduced at the end of the 17th century, and not repealed until 1851. The amount of tax paid depended on the *number* of windows in the house, and between 1746 and 1808 window taxes were increased six times. The Treasury's coffers may have been swelled, but the levies and taxes kept the less well-off in continuing dark and ill-ventilated houses. Often they could not afford to replace the glass in the few windows they did have, and blocked the holes with rags or paper.

While it is true that some home owners bricked up a few of their windows to avoid paying the tax, the blocked windows often to be seen in old houses are not always the result of this. Sometimes architects would incorporate dummy windows merely to preserve the symmetry of design, and in other cases a re-arrangement of the house's internal features – with perhaps a new staircase or passageway – led to the closing of some original windows.

The aristocracy and the gentry, who set the fashions in architecture, continued to demand bigger and bigger windows for their houses during the 18th century. The size of each pane of glass was, however, still constrained by production techniques: crown glass panels could seldom be satisfactorily made much bigger than 10 inches across.

Although plate glass, rolled into larger panels was first produced at St. Helens in Lancashire in 1773 it was not until the abolition of taxes and duties in the mid-19th century that it began to come into widespread use. But once cheap, good-quality plate glass was available, there was no stopping it. Glazing bars could be dispensed with, the whole window area being replaced with glass. Whilst this undoubtedly meant that more light was let into the house, windows became less aesthetically pleasing, losing the pattern and proportion of glazing bars or lead cames.

FRAMES FOR WINDOWS

The earliest windows were little more than holes in the wall, designed for ventilation. The Romans did bring with them more sophisticated techniques, introducing windows topped with semi-circular arches. With the Dark Ages, however, most of the techniques of the Romans were lost and it was not until the conversion of the country to Christianity, and the beginnings of church building, that architecture again revived.

The Saxons built principally in wood so few traces of their secular buildings remain, but in their stone churches we can find clues to the methods they used to frame their windows. Late Saxon church windows were often based on half-forgotten Roman techniques. The true arch, it seems, was beyond the skill of the early Saxon builder but there are church windows which mimic an arch, their solid stone lintels carved on the underside. In other Saxon church windows there were merely two stones leaning against each other, resting on the sill to produce a triangular opening; or even more basic, a solid stone slab pierced with a small circular hole.

Saxon windows are all small, due not just to a lack of technical skill, but also to defensive needs and because the desire was not primarily for internal light but for ventilation. In their wooden halls and barns the Saxons usually placed their windows at the gable ends (the roofs coming too low at the eaves to allow windows in the side walls). A stone slab with a small hole bored through might be used to close the opening, or a slab of timber 2 or 3 inches thick, perforated with a series of holes and fitted centrally into the width of the wall.

Shutters would also be used. At first they were probably removable and merely pushed into the opening at night, but the Saxons also used the method of hanging a swinging shutter on a pivot or *harr* which slotted into the sill and the lintel. Such window openings and shutters may seem very crude, but in them we can see the beginnings of windows as we know them today: the pierced stone slab showed an early form of the masonic skill that was to develop into the elegant tracery of the Gothic period; the perforated oak plank evolved into the window frame; the pivoted shutter was the first step towards the side-hung casement window.

By the late Saxon period, small arched windows were being built in churches, and double arches developed, the centre being supported on a stone column. The Normans had similar styles but were more accomplished builders in stone and could span much wider apertures. They

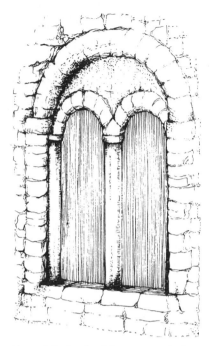 

Above left: In the Norman period new building techniques enabled the arched window to develop.

Above right: Early Gothic windows were tall and thin. The style developed into double and triple windows, culminating in the delicate tracery and elaborate patterns of the Decorated style. During the Gothic Revival of Victorian times, Gothic style windows were once again favoured.

used stone, too, in their secular buildings, in their halls and manor houses, and their windows were in the same style as those of their churches, for there was no real division between church and domestic architecture.

Gothic Windows

The 13th century saw the beginning of Gothic architecture, and the replacement of the rounded romanesque arch with a pointed one, as used in the great cathedrals. Early Gothic windows were tall and thin, and when larger lights were needed they would be grouped in twos or threes. As the style progressed a further arch was added to surround such groups and the stonework became progressively more intricate, culminating in the delicate tracery and elaborate patterns of the Decorated style. Again the castles and the larger houses followed the fashions of church architecture, but for the ordinary man's home there was little change: the cottage still had a hole in the roof for a chimney and a small unglazed opening for a window. Some shutters, however, were now 'top-hung' and held open by a prop during the day.

The Decorated style gradually gave way to the Perpendicular in the 15th century, with tall, wide church windows with slender mullions and numerous lights which were often divided by thin horizontal transoms as well. The halls and manor houses had by now lost their fortified character and they adopted and adapted the ecclesiastical styles. Bay windows also made their appearance; and oriels, many-sided windows jutting out, usually from an upper storey.

Casement Windows

The 15th century, too, saw the introduction of the iron casement window: a frame of wrought iron, hinged at the side, and glazed with small panes jointed with lead cames. There were vertical and horizontal reinforcing rods for added strength and the leaded lights were wired to these for support. The casement was the prototype of the modern window, but again it should be emphasised that its use was limited to the great houses, manors and Halls and to the town houses of the new breed of wealthy merchants.

Fresh air was not much valued in the Middle Ages. On the contrary it was believed that the wind, particularly from the south, brought pestilence with it – a suspicion confirmed in many people's mind by the Black Death of the middle of the 14th century, which started in Dorset and spread rapidly up through the country, ultimately killing about one third of the entire population. Wherever possible houses were aligned north/south (often even if the village street ran east/west) so their narrow and windowless ends faced the dreaded south wind.

In Tudor times much more attention was being paid to domestic architecture. In the brick-built houses of this period the windows were set in stone surrounds, with stone mullions and transoms while windows in the best timber-framed houses tended to reflect in wood the architectural styles of the stonemasons. In the smaller houses and cottages, however, windows remained simple affairs with the horizontal timbers – the lintel and the sill – jointed into the vertical studs of the wall. The opening was often protected by thin vertical mullions, acting as 'burglar bars', square or diamond-shaped in section. Shutters were still the rule rather than the exception, either hinged or sliding in grooves. It seems

During the great rebuilding of the 16th century mullioned windows, set in stone or iron frames, were fashionable and continued to be widely used up until the 18th century. The small glass panes were usually joined together with lead cames into the familiar diamond pattern.

likely that the movable, glazed, wooden-frame window developed as a replacement of the grooved shutter; and as we have seen, these were regarded more or less as items of furniture, to be taken away on moving house, rather than fixtures and fittings. A few of the shutters or glazed frames seen to have slide vertically. In 1519, for example, a William Horman wrote: 'I have many pretty wyndowes shette with louys going up and down'. This is one of the earliest references to a vertical sash-type arrangement, a style for windows that was to gain widespread popularity in the 17th and 18th centuries.

While we can chart the introduction of new styles and development in windows, it should be remembered that the old styles continued to be used for centuries in the smaller houses and cottages. The forms of windows introduced in medieval times – either a series of thin arched windows, or a squared-off timber-frame divided by mullions – continued in use until the end of the 17th century. What is known as the 'sub-medieval phase', a transition between the older series of narrow mullioned 'lights' and the tall, well-proportioned sash window, lasted well into the 18th century in smaller houses, and was still being used for buildings like workshops in the mid-19th century.

'Sub-medieval' windows were much squarer in outline than earlier ones. When the window was in stone it was usually divided in two by a thin mullion, although this was often removed at a later date when new window frames were put in. In brick, windows would have a shallow arch on top and the space was divided into two, or sometimes three, lights by slender wooden mullions. Alternatively the whole window might be divided into rectangular sections with horizontal and vertical glazing bars.

In timber-frame houses, as less wood began to be used in the walls, windows became independent of the wall timbers, having their own jambs instead of the lintels and sills being slotted into the vertical stud work.

The design of mullions changed over the years, the ones made in wood generally reflecting the styles of stone but usually being lighter in section. Early mullions had straight splays (the uprights) but these were super-seded by splays with a hollowed out section, giving a much lighter effect. This form is typical of late 16th and early 17th century windows. In the late 17th century, ovolo mouldings became popular. These had a convex shape, with square fillets.

Windows that opened, at least in part, were becoming commoner by the 16th and 17th centuries, with side-hung casements in iron or wood making up one half of the squarish opening.

Another development was the 'Yorkshire' sash, very popular in that part of the country but spreading elsewhere too. Here, a half of the window slid open horizontally, running in grooves top and bottom. But again the smaller dwellings, if they were glazed at all, generally had fixed windows with perhaps just one small pane that opened.

By the 17th century the influence of the Renaissance was beginning to be seen in domestic architecture, and its classical lines were reflected in the windows which, from being squarish, now became taller rectangles. The mullion and transom were often arranged in the form of a cross, so that the upper lights were smaller than the lower ones. The glass pieces were still usually jointed together with lead cames but the traditional diagonal pattern of these gave way to a rectangular one, more in keeping with the lines of the window frame and surrounds.

Sash Windows

Perhaps the greatest revolution of all in window design came in the late 17th and early 18th centuries with the introduction into Britain of the vertical sliding sash, made in wood. It is not absolutely clear where it came from but it is generally accepted as a Dutch innovation; the Dutch were certainly responsible for many improvements in house building techniques at this time. In the earliest sashes, the upper half of the window was usually fixed, only the lower section sliding up and down. Later both upper and lower sections were movable and smooth opening and closing was ensured by a system of pulleys and counterweights hidden within the window frame.

In earlier sash windows the wooden frames were usually fitted flush with the wall's outer surface, but wooden windows were considered a great fire hazard, especially in towns, and the London Building Acts in 1707 and 1709 required that they be set back 4 inches from the walls. This style was adopted in some other places too, although in many areas the sash remained flush with the wall. Another trend in design was towards narrower and narrower glazing bars; by the beginning of the 19th century they had become very thin indeed.

The tall rectangular window remained popular throughout all the changes in design of the English house: in classic Georgian windows and through the Greek and Gothic revivals of the 18th and 19th centuries. There were variations in style, of course, such as the elegant 'Palladian' or 'Cribbs' window which gave more light to staircase landings. Here there was a central arched light with narrower square-headed lights on either side. In the Gothic revival, rounded or arched windows were reintroduced, but now both upper and lower sections slid vertically. Another Gothic style was to place two light, square-headed windows side by side topped by a common moulding on the wall. Often glazing bars were completely eliminated, particularly in the mid-19th century as larger sheets of plate glass became available.

The outside mouldings above windows added much to the pleasing appearance of houses. Originally such 'hood' or 'weather' moulds were purely functional: to protect the window opening from rain-water running down the wall surface. Soon, however, they were also regarded as decorative features, arched or square-head mouldings complementing the overall house design. Groups of windows were often linked by a continuous moulding: ultimately such mouldings ran the length of the walls, marking the level of the storeys. Window surrounds in brick-built houses, too, were used to enhance design, with contrasting-coloured brick dressings around them. Arched lintels were given projecting key-

The sash window was a revolution in window design in the 17th century. This example from the Georgian era of the 18th century shows the hood, decorative mouldings and embellishments which enhanced the appearance of houses of that time.

stones, often carved. While this was common in the 17th and early 18th centuries, it became less widespread later as the trend was to simpler facades.

In rural areas and particularly in the north of England, the tradition of mullioned windows never died away entirely and in some cases timber sashes were fitted between the mullions, replacing the iron frames and leaded lights. But while the vertical sash ousted all rivals from the better houses – particularly those of brick, or stucco-covered, or timber-clad – for the house built in stone and for the smaller country cottage, the side-hung casement or the horizontally-sliding sash were still preferred. These were used to replace the older mullioned windows in many a smaller house and cottage and were not only cheaper to construct but better suited to the squatter window openings in such houses. In the country too, cast-iron casements divided into small panes were a popular replacement for the timber frame. The village blacksmith added their construction to his skills.

By the middle of the 19th century, with the Industrial Revolution in full swing, both iron and bigger sheets of glass were being produced in large quantities and architects used them to glaze large areas, both in public buildings, like the 1851 Crystal Palace and the terminii for the new railways, and in conservatories, so fashionable for the Victorian family house. Factory-made wrought-iron window frames were appearing too, often with elaborate designs of curve and tracery.

Today factory-made windows are available in a variety of materials and styles: sash and casement, 'Georgian' and even leaded lights. But restoration work and replacement of old windows can be a tricky business.

Dormer Windows

The introduction of the chimney stack and the 'chambering over' of Hall houses heralded the beginning of everyday two-storey living. But there were problems in lighting and ventilating the newly-created first-floor rooms. There was generally little space for a window, since the walls were fairly low and only a few feet of them rose into the upper floor. Building technology was not advanced enough to provide waterproof skylights in the sloping sides of the roof, so the solution was the dormer window, set vertically under its own miniature roof, pitched at right angles to the main one. The upper rooms, with their inclined ceilings, could really only be used for sleeping and the word dormer derives from the Latin *dormitorium* or sleeping-room.

The commonest form of dormer roof is a pitched inverted V, but another technique was to raise the ends of some of the rafters in the main roof and rest them over the top of the window. In thatch areas, the roof-covering was then swept over the irregular frame of rafters, producing a pleasing curved effect and what are known as 'eyebrow' windows. When tiles were used on roofs, the sections over the raised rafters above the dormer window are known at 'catslides'.

With the pitched dormer roof there are waterproofing problems in the angles where it meets the main roof. With thatch this could be overcome without much difficulty by weaving together the reed or straw to provide a continuous covering, and with stone tiles the courses could be laid to sweep neatly over the joints. In plain tiled roofs, the 'valley' was filled with specially shaped tiles, but for slates and pantiles, lead strips were required at the junctions.

The style of the dormer roof echoed that of the main one – being hipped if the roof was hipped, gabled if it was gabled; but the position of the dormer varied considerably. It might be on the eaves line, set lower (beginning in the wall itself), or it might be placed wholly in the roof slope. There are distinct regional variations. The characteristic Cotswold dormer, for instance, has a steeply-pointed gable, a straight continuation of the front wall above the eaves. In areas where Dutch gables were popular, the dormer surround would follow this style in a reduced form, and dormers in Georgian houses reflected the classical embellishments seen around the doors and windows.

While the building of dormer windows began in the Middle Ages and they continued to be widely used in the 16th and 17th centuries, it was in the 18th that they really came into their own, especially in the eastern counties where agriculture was thriving. Farms were growing in size and in production and more labour was needed. The workers slept in the attic rooms, lit by a row of dormer windows. In the towns too, where building room was increasingly scarce, dormers in the roof enabled more space to be used.

Just as today loft extensions provide extra rooms, so too house owners through the centuries have extended their living space, and many a dormer is actually an addition to a house rather than part of the original building. It is sometimes difficult to tell this in houses built before the 18th century; after this period as dormers became widespread, it is more than likely that they are original.

WINDOW REPAIR AND RESTORATION

Painting

As with many others parts of the house, the main cause of trouble with windows is damp. A regular protective coat of paint is the answer, to prevent the damp penetrating into the wood and setting up the conditions for rot to develop. If re-painted every couple of years or so, a well-made timber window will last for a considerable time, possibly indefinitely. Since paint itself is attacked by sunlight and by heat, particular attention should be paid to south-facing windows.

With the introduction of chimney stacks, the roof space could be floored over, thus creating an upper storey which could be used for accommodation with the addition of a dormer window set into the roof. From the 18th century dormer windows were built as an integral part of newly-built cottages.

Examine your windows regularly for signs of paint peeling away or chipped off. If the damage is slight, all that will be needed is a smoothing off with glass-paper and a new top coat applied. With more extensive flaking and peeling it is better to strip back to the wood, either by burning off the paint or by using a proprietary paint stripper, and then apply at least three good protective layers, of primer, undercoat and top coat.

Restoration
If the previous owners were less than fastidious in the protection of their exterior woodwork there will almost certainly be some deterioration of the wood through rotting. It is not possible to make this sound and the only sensible course is to remove the rotten area and replace it. Where the damage is extensive, it is better, despite the cost, to remove and replace the whole window frame.

In old houses this can prove to be an expensive business, especially if the original windows are of a unique and sophisticated design. A replica will have to be made up by a professional joiner so that the new window is in keeping with the others. Ready-made window frames can be bought in all shapes and sizes, but most mass-produced frames tend to be heavier and clumsier than earlier hand-crafted ones and look terribly out of place. Incidentally, if your house is a listed building, then you cannot make a change in window frames without obtaining consent from your local authority planning department.

Window sills

Window sills are generally made of hardwood, and tend to be more durable than the rest of the frame. They need to be, of course, because they take the brunt of the water. Check them regularly, for damage, particularly underneath, not only to make sure the paint looks sound but also, by pressing with the thumb, to feel if the wood has gone spongy. The sill has a groove underneath, to keep the water away from the wall, so make sure this has not become blocked.

If there is not a great deal of decay, the sill can be renovated by a dressing sheet of lead. Localised rot can be cured by cutting away the offending area and grafting in a new piece of hardwood before repainting. Again, however, if the damage is extensive, it is better to remove and replace the whole sill. Sometimes this can be done without having to take out the window, but more often than not because of the window's construction, it will involve major surgery.

There can be problems with the internal sills too, particularly in old houses where central heating has been installed. The warm dry air can cause the wood to shrink, creating a gap between window frame and sill. There are many proprietary plastic fillers on the market today which should overcome subsequent problems of shrinking and cracking.

Sash and sliding windows

Sash and sliding windows are often of complicated construction and design and things can easily go wrong. The commonest complaint is that they stick – a fault to which Yorkshire sashes are particularly prone, especially during a wet season when the wood expands. A bit of candle wax in the channels often works, otherwise the only remedy is to take out the sliding section and carefully smooth away small amounts of wood so that the window will glide easily in its channels. Repainting any bits of exposed wood will stop further water penetration.

Vertical sliding sashes also run into mechanical problems. All too familiar is the breaking of the sash cord.

If you are no handyman, it might be advisable to get someone professional to do the job, for it can be a little tricky – and frustrating.

Reglazing

If you have to replace the windows, it is always worth saving the old glass and using it in the new frames. Crown glass particularly should be conserved, as it is irreplaceable and its slight imperfections add much to the character of a window.

Double glazing presents a dilemma for the owner of an old house. It obviously makes sense to cut back on heating bills by eliminating draughts and reducing heat loss. Our own inclination, if the old windows in the house are good is not to double glaze but to concentrate on roof insulation and making sure the windows are draught-free. They are likely to be smaller than modern ones so heat loss should be less.

There are many double glazing systems on the market, some of them purporting to provide double glazed replicas of period windows. If you do decide to use them, choose with great care and remember that they are unlikely to have the delicacy of design of the originals.

A simple but effective double glazing method is to fit large framed sheets of acrylic plastics over the inside of the entire window opening. This means that no additional glazing bars can be seen from the outside. The sheets can be removed in summer, so that you can then enjoy your house the traditional way, with the windows open.

Opening up old windows

Second only to the joy of discovery and opening up an old fireplace is the restoration of an old blocked-up window. In timber-framed houses particularly, the original mullions of a blocked up window will probably still be there, even though the window frame has been filled in with wattle and daub or brick. Restoring a window and glazing it sensitively will add a very pleasing feature to the house, and give some sense of its original appearance.

We said at the beginning of this chapter that windows are a house's eyes, they add so much to its character. So it is vital in window restoration or replacement to proceed with the greatest care. If you have any doubts, consult an architect with experience in restoration or get in touch with your local council's Architects Department who should have plenty of practical advice.

Doors

An ancient way to describe an intended visit to someone was to say that you were going to 'darken his door', a phrase that is still used in angry dismissal: 'Never darken my door again!'. It was accurate symbolism, for in our earliest houses the doorway was not only the way of going in and out, but also the sole source of light for the gloomy windowless interiors. It would be left open during the day and blocked temporarily at night, perhaps by an animal hide, by a lattice of wattle, or even by building up stone slabs.

EARLY DOORS

As houses improved, however, it soon became clear that something better than cowhide or wattle was needed to cover the doorway. The standard solution was to butt together a series of vertical planks and secure them with two or three internal horizontal cross-members or ledges. The odd diagonal plank or two might be added for further stability or, in another variation, an extra-stout, double-thickness door could be made with an outer layer of vertical planks and an inner layer of horizontal ones (battens), the two secured to each other with pegs, either of wood or of metal. A few of the plank-and-ledge medieval doors still exist, some with added character given by fillets covering the vertical joints, but most have long since vanished. Throughout the centuries, however, the basic technique continued to be used for more menial doors, and even today you will find the doors of garages and garden sheds constructed in this way.

The early doors were heavy affairs, generally made of hardwood, usually oak. Since it would clearly have been troublesome to heave them daily into and out of position, they hinged at the side. The earliest device was a simple strap of metal around the door, slotting over a vertical pin in the wall opening. Since at first there was no door frame as such, the pin was fixed straight into the wall – either into the stone surround or into one of the vertical studs of a timber framed house.

In shape, the top of the doorway showed many variations. It might be square-headed or in an arched curve, reflecting the style of the period and

The door of the Jew's House, Lincoln, was exceptionally fine for the 12th century. Most ordinary houses had a plain wood door fixed on a strap and pin fastening.

reiterating the detail of the window surrounds. In the 14th and 15th centuries, the two-centred arch was popular, but by the late 15th, the four-centred arch has appeared, a shape that continued to be used well into the 17th century, gradually becoming flatter. Other variations include the ogee and the shouldered arch. Mouldings above the door to stave off rainwater repeated those above the windows, except at their ends where mason or carpenter would add decorated stops or corbels. Later in the medieval period drip courses all along the wall were introduced following the line of window and another variant is a horizontal drip mould with 'dropped and returned ends'.

There were intriguing regional differences in the size of the doors in medieval houses. They were all generally a little lower than modern doors, which is not surprising since people were shorter; and by and large they were more or less the same width as we would expect today; between 2 ft 10 inches and 3 ft. But in some parts of England, notably in the West Country, the doors were often much wider, and no one really knows why this should be.

Another characteristic of the West, and of Wales too, was the early introduction of a proper door frame, something that was not to become widespread until the 16th century. Having the door hinged on strap and pin meant that it did not fit perfectly and the wind whistled coldly through the cracks. The door frame covered these, cutting out the draughts. To obtain an even better fit, doors needed a neater hanging arrangement. The answer was the hinge – and its design and manufacture became another skill of the local blacksmith. Hinges came in all sorts of shapes and sizes, from simple L-and H-shaped ones to intricate and highly-decorated designs. The weight of the door, however, meant that they had to be much sturdier than those of today, which gives them a certain charm and makes them well worth retaining as a feature in older houses.

Early doors had other pieces of monumental ironmongery attached to them. There might be a wrought-iron grill set in, an early 'spy-hole' to monitor callers, and the door would be secured at night with a heavy draw-bar slotted into brackets on the wall or door frame. This was later replaced or augmented with a stout lock: these again were at first much bigger and clumsier than modern designs, and were fitted with the large keys that have now become popular collectors' items.

By the 15th century plank and ledge doors fixed with iron hinges onto a snugly fitting door frame made houses more secure and comfortable.

The early 17th century saw the introduction of the panelled door, giving scope for more variety in design and decoration.

PANELLED DOORS

The heavy doorways of medieval, Tudor and Elizabethan times were uneconomical in their use of wood and the increasing shortage of timber in the 17th century led to the introduction of the panelled door: while preserving the strength of the older varieties, this used less wood. The door consists of an open frame strengthened with a few horizontal and vertical cross-members, with the gaps between filled with thinner wooden panels. It requires greater carpentry skills, of course, but the result is more aesthetically pleasing and gives added scope for variety in design and decoration. Six-panelled doors were commonplace in the 18th century, the upper pair being relatively small and the middle pair the largest; but later doors were made with more panels of differing sizes and shapes, such as the eight-panelled one, arranged in rows of – starting at the top – two, three, one and two panels.

The panels themselves could be flat or raised ('fielded' is the technical term) and they slotted into grooves in the door frame and cross-members. The look of the door was further enhanced by shaping the timbers and by the addition of decorative mouldings, which also concealed any gap between panel and door member.

The classical Georgian door, easily identified by its columns and elaborate pediments.

The introduction of the panelled door meant that lighter hinges could be used and it also led to the introduction of butt hinges, which are concealed between the door and its outer frame. They are the standard fixtures for modern doors.

TUDOR, ELIZABETHAN AND GEORGIAN DOORS

By late Tudor and early Elizabethan times the doorway was well on the way to becoming one of the principal architectural features of the house, particularly of larger properties. Often it was set in an outer hallway or porch that carried on upwards to the full height of the building. The woodwork or stone was intricately carved, and by the end of this period classical details were beginning to appear.

In some parts of the country, notably in the stone-building area around the Lake District and the Pennines, examples can still be found of doorways which are really a curious hybrid of earlier styles with glimmerings of the Renaissance and neo-Classicism. Stone lintels are common and it was popular to carve their undersides to represent a four-centred arch. Later the lintels would be more intricately carved, and decorated with dates, initials and heraldic devices. Mouldings above the doorway would mimic battlements or arches and, later still, the whole upper doorway would begin to take on the classical look of the Renaissance.

In the classical revival the doorway reached its zenith as an architectural feature, and even doors in smaller houses reflected the influence of the new ideas in art and architecture. Canopies and pediments were the order of the day by the late 17th and early 18th centuries. Square-headed door surrounds were commonest, particularly early on, but the style developed into a variety of shapes, sizes and decorations. There were triangular pediments and curved ones, pediments shaped like scrolls, pediments broken and enhanced with a central decoration. The semi-circular arch was popular too, with a large keystone often initialled and dated, and also the square-headed doorway surmounted by a lintel to imitate stepped voussoirs (the wedge-shaped blocks of an arch).

In all but the humblest houses the front door opened into a hall, or at least a porch, and this was lit by a fanlight above the door, usually semi-circular in shape. Nowhere can this flowering of the door's development be better seen than in the houses put up in London's building boom in the 18th century, not only in elaborate pediments and cornices and delicate low reliefs, but also in the classical columns that now commonly surrounded the door – some squared, some rounded, others reflecting the full vigour of the Doric and Ionic orders.

The doors themselves were more often than not of six panels and generally made in pine or deal, which was painted. Richer houses, however, might still have hardwood doors, notably in mahogany veneer.

The classical doorway eventually fell from fashion, not least because of a succession of Building Acts in London, which discouraged the use of projecting timber work on facades. The door began to merge back into its surrounding wall, although the opening was still emphasised with ornamental masonry or brickwork. The proper outer hall, or porch, receded too, although in the later 18th century its place was often taken by a trellis-like open structure of ornamental cast iron – a fashionable addition both to newly-built houses and to older properties.

VICTORIAN AND MODERN DOORS

With the rapid development of glassmaking techniques of the 19th century, sheets of glass began to make their appearance in doors, at first replacing the wood in the upper two panels but later used in a single large panel which took up most of the upper half of the door. So that it still let in light but prevented the glances of the curious, the glass would be etched with acid, or coloured, and in the latter case often with a geometric pattern of panes. Such doors tended to be out of fashion in the 20th century and were replaced, but if they do still remain in a Victorian house, they are worth retaining, renovating and repainting. It might prove a little difficult to find the glass, but there are still specialised firms which should be able to help.

Domestic architecture in the 20th century has seen such a bewildering variety of styles and revivals that it is impossible to generalise about developments with doors. Medieval-style plank doors, with metal studs, showed up again in many a suburban development, as did doors with leaded lights, perhaps with coloured sun-bursts or curious Art Deco designs, popular in the 1930s. Also making its mark in the 1920s (although there are earlier examples) was the glazed or French door, almost totally of glass and usually with 15 panes, arranged in five rows of three. While it was occasionally used as a front door, it found most favour in the double version – a pair of french windows leading out into the garden. In the 1960s and 1970s the Georgian door made a comeback, even in small houses with no other pretentions to classical symmetry. Today, however, householders seem able to choose a new front door from most periods of history in many different veneers of wood.

Glass in doors made its appearance in early Victorian times and by the mid 19th century it was often coloured in geometric patterna of panes.

DOOR FURNITURE

Early doors, as we have seen, would be 'furnished' on the inside with a draw-bar and perhaps also a large lock, while on the outside the straps of the hinges could be seen, with also a key hole and possibly a pattern of metal studs. Locks later evolved so that they could be fitted within the thickness of the door itself, something that is commonplace today. But two other items of door furniture are comparatively recent additions – the door knocker and the letter box. Knobs, knockers and handles evolved in the 18th century, and although the very best were in brass, they were usually made in cast iron, and painted. So if you want your house to look authentic, there is really no need to go to all the bother – and expense – of brass, although it seems that few people can resist it. Whatever 'furniture' you fit, though, take care that it suits the shape and symmetry of the door.

Floors and Ceilings

For hundreds of years – even up to the 18th century in the lowliest houses – the ground floor of the house was simply beaten earth. While neither clean or hygienic by modern standards, a well-laid floor can provide a surprisingly solid surface, not all that dissimilar to concrete. The secret lay in the preparation of the ground and in the mixing-in of certain natural additives with the earth, to meld it together. The basic technique was to dig over the ground and rake the earth painstakingly to produce a tilth as fine as that in a seed bed. Then gallon upon gallon of water would be poured over it and the resulting quagmire allowed to drain, settle and dry, a process that might take as long as a month, but which resulted in a hard compacted skin to the floor, with a texture rather like baked mud. This would be uneven, so the final task was *melling*, beating the floor flat with wooden paddles.

Among the additives mixed with the earth to make it even more solid and durable were lime (which was used from earlier medieval times in districts where it was readily available), sand, bone chips and fine clay. Bulls' blood was sometimes used too, to give a dense dark surface which could even be polished.

Despite the maker's best endeavours, though, beaten earth floors were dusty and in an effort to keep this down, especially in summer, they were strewn with straw, rushes or grasses. If this covering was changed regularly when it dried out or began to smell too much, then the floors could be kept clean and tidy. But the 16th century English, it seems, were far from fastidious in this, judging by a letter written by Erasmus, who stayed in Britain in the early 1500s. He told a friend: 'The floors are commonly of clay, strewed with rushes, under which lies unmolested an ancient collection of beer, grease, fragments, bones, spittle, excrement of dogs and cats and everything that is nasty.' There was obviously some nastiness seeping into the floors, not only from cat and dog excrement but from human urine as well, for our ancestors were not too bothered about sanitation. Whatever its source, the result was that the floors soaked up material rich in nitre – the 'saltpetre' used in making gun-powder. Since this was scarce, the Crown turned to floors as a rich source of much-needed war material, and empowered 'saltpetre men' to enter people's homes, dig up and take away their floors. The Crown was supposed to make good any damage but, as this was seldom done, the visits of the saltpetre men were far from welcome, especially as they also had powers to remove earth walls – those of cob, for instance – if necessary. It was not until the Commonwealth period that the saltpetre men's powers of 'common seisin' were revoked.

Gradually, and as usual starting with better-class homes, earthen floors were replaced with more solid covering. Stone slabs were used in those areas where suitable rock was in good supply; elsewhere alternatives had to be found, such as brick and clay tiles, which were in common use for floors by the 17th century. Early floor tiles were larger than those of today and were unglazed; glazed tiles were an 18th century development, which saw full flowering in the magnificent mosaic tiles used in striking patterns in Georgian and Victorian entrance halls.

In the 18th century, timber floors were brought in for living rooms, stone and tiles being retained only in kitchens and other service rooms, such as the laundry.

UPPER FLOORS

Owing to the fact that the top section of medieval houses was filled with smoke from the fire burning in the central hearth (see Fireplaces p 151), whole upper floors were uncommon before the 14th century, although wings with upstairs rooms called solars, which afforded some privacy from the communal hurly-burly of the hall, were often constructed at one end of the house (or less commonly at both ends). Their flooring was of wooden boards resting on flat joists, which could be decoratively carved or moulded. It was not normal at this period to plaster the underside of floors, so boards and joists were visible as the ceiling of the room below.

The development of proper chimneys from the 15th century onwards removed the smoke from the upper part of the hall and meant that extra accommodation could be provided by a complete 'flooring over' or 'chambering over'. By careful investigation it is possible to tell if a floor was a later addition to the house, or whether it was put in during the original building. If the roof is original then there will be traces of sooty deposits on its beams and rafters, from the fires that would have burned almost continuously in the open hearth below.

In Wealden houses (see p 16), found principally in the south of England, the central section would certainly have been a single storey hall open to the roof, so upper floors must be a later addition. For other types it is sometimes more difficult to find out, although for the discerning eye there are differences in the quality of the timber between the floor joists and supporting beams, and those of the wall beams and studs. And study the joints between the main beam of the ceiling and wall timbers. If the beam has been added later the carpenters would have had problems in squeezing it into position, so the joint will generally be less snug than if the beam was put in when the house was built.

There are those purists who, on discovering the first floor is a later addition, have removed it to restore the hall to its medieval proportions. This is fine if you do not need the accommodation, but hardly necessary; the first floor was a welcome innovation, adding convenience and comfort to the house.

One of the curious techniques of medieval carpenters, who possessed considerable woodworking skills, was that they laid their floor joists flat, rather than upright. So the joists were rather like narrow planks, with the floorboards fixed above them. Since wood was plentiful, the joists – normally of oak – could be set close together, perhaps with no more than a foot between their centres, so the floor above would be sturdy enough, but it would be springy and move when walked on. It was not until the 17th century, it seems, that carpenters realised that the floor could be considerably strengthened by turning the joists on edge or using timbers that were square in section. The move to this technique was no doubt accelerated by the use of softwood joists, as good hardwood became scarcer. Where flat joists met wall timbers the joints would creak; so when the upper floor was being used the medieval house was a noisy place. The problem was overcome, no doubt unintentionally, by the fashion for 'jettying' the upper storeys, a technique imported from the continent in the 14th century and widely used from the 15th to the 17th centuries. The floor joists were extended beyond the ground floor-walls built up from these protruding edges. The jetty might be constructed on just one side of the house, or two, or even on all four – and it is a form that is one of the most recognisable features of later medieval, Tudor and Elizabethan timber-frame houses.

All sorts of reasons have been put forward for jettying: that it gave more space in the upper storey rooms; that it strengthened the floor by cantilevering the joists and generally helped the carpenter to construct a firmly jointed timber framework; that it gave more protection against the weather for the lower floors. All this is true – space in upper rooms, for instance, could be increased by as much as 20 per cent and this must have been an important consideration in crowded towns – but the advantages seem to be a consequence of jettying rather than its *raison*

In timber buildings with an upper storey, jettying on two adjacent sides was made possible by using dragon beams, protruding from the house corner into which the floor joists would be jointed.

d'etre. Most likely medieval and Tudor builders constructed jettied houses because they were pleasing to the eye and were fashionable. Jettying was certainly not essential and in fact the majority of houses in this period were built with straight walls.

At first jetties often extended only at the front of the house, or at front and back, since the joists ran at right angles to the frontage, but jettying of three or four walls was made possible by the use of the dragon beam, a substantial diagonal joist protruding from the house corner. (The word 'dragon' is probably a corruption of diagonal.)

The first floor could be further strengthened, and its span increased, by the use of a massive central ceiling beam, into which the joists were tenoned. Such beams are called summers or summer trees, the word deriving from the Anglo-Norman *somer,* itself a derivative of the Latin and Greek words for pack-horse. And that is apt, for the summer takes the load of the ceiling and the upper floor on its back. It commonly ran from wall to chimney breast and – though the accompanying joists may have been plastered over – usually the summer was left exposed, its lines frequently softened by chamfering and carved and moulded designs. The shape and style of such details can give useful clues to dating the house. Contrary to the general rule, the decoration of summer, joist and 'stop moulds' at the joints seems to get less elaborate as time goes on.

Floorboards were originally planks of oak or elm, although when good wood became scarce and increased in price, cheaper alternatives

138

such as pine and deal were used. Also, as a general rule, floorboards have become narrower over the centuries, early examples being a foot or more in width. Until well into the 19th century the boards were merely butted together: tongue-and-groove boarding is a comparatively recent innovation.

Wood was not the only material used for upper floors, although it was the commonest. Plaster, earth, even stone were used too. Despite the large size of the timber joists required to support the weight of stone upper floors, these were built as late as the Georgian period.

Floors of plaster were especially prevalent in the East Midlands, not only in smaller houses but in quite superior ones as well. The use of plaster was due in part to timber shortages, but some builders suggested it gave a better, more even finish which would not warp or settle. The floor joists, and supporting beams where necessary, were laid in the same way as for floorboards, but then a bed of straw or reeds was laid across them over which was trowelled a covering of plaster, as much as 2 inches thick. The best ingredient for the plaster was gypsum, although lime was also used, particularly in the Cotswolds. Clay or burnt brick were added as the aggregate. Plaster, however, while being strong in compression is weaker in tension, and plaster floors had a tendency to crack when heavy loads, like the bed or old oak chest, were put on them. Earth or mud upper floors were occasionally made in areas where gypsum or lime were hard to come by, but they tended to be relegated to less important areas like lofts.

CEILINGS

A favourite expression of estate agents selling old houses is 'with a wealth of exposed timbers'. Very fine such houses look, but it is important to remember that, as with the timber in walls, not all ceiling beams and joists were meant to be exposed. In the better quality medieval houses, joist and summer, and the underside of the floorboards, were left uncovered, but where the joists were of rough-hewn timber there would have been some covering-up. This was done by packing the space between the joists with a filling of clay and straw, which was then plastered over.

By the 16th century the owners of better-quality homes were demanding plastered ceilings, both for the sake of appearance and for insulation, and by the 18th century this was the rule rather than the exception in all but the smallest houses and cottages. Also, the process of modernisation of old properties continued and even those ceilings with fine

By the 16th century owners of better quality houses led the fashion for covering the ceiling beams and joists behind a false ceiling. It was then plastered and ornamented like this Elizabethan example.

decorated oak beams and joists which were intended to be on show were covered over with a layer of plaster. There are even cases where a whole false ceiling, with its own supporting joists, was suspended beneath the first floor, so the deep summers could be hidden beneath a smooth surface. The basis for the plaster was a series of laths nailed to the underside of the joists. At first these were 'riven', split by hand, but by the 19th century sawn laths came into use, so examining these can give another clue to dating.

Early builders also often put insulation between the ceiling and the first floor, using chaff and straw between the joists, which not only increased the fire risk but provided a cosy haven for rats and mice.

The substances used in the plaster varied from area to area, but a popular recipe was a mix of lime and sand with cowhair added for binding strength. Gypsum, which is widely used today, was at first confined to areas where it occurred naturally, in the East Midlands, for instance. Decorators were unable to resist the extra opportunities that plaster gave them to show off their skills and from the late 17th century particularly there are many fine examples of decorative work and intricate mouldings, especially in friezes.

When restoring old property it is common practice to expose the timber beams, and this invariably produces a pleasing effect, even if they were not originally intended to be seen. One of the hazards of this task is the evil black dust that emanates if that old-fashioned insulation was used; but one of the joys of discovering chamfered and decorated summers and joists that may have been hidden for generations.

Repairs and renovations

The new owner of an old house may well find that his floors are worn and decayed. Earthen floors have all but disappeared, covered over with brick and tile, but even these more substantial coverings are subject to wear and tear, especially where there has been a heavy passage of feet over the years. Before ripping up an old floor, however, and replacing it with a modern damp-proofed concrete base, it is wise to pause for thought. Fitted carpets over concrete can be perfectly in keeping with an old house, but nothing can enhance it more than having at least a principal room or two floored in traditional materials.

One of the delights of ancient floor tiles – and old bricks, too – was that they were hand-made; it is their subtle variations in colour that give old floors such a pleasing look. Modern machine-made floor tiles are uniform, so this effect is lost; and even replacing only the very worn or broken old tiles with new ones is seldom a satisfactory solution. It is worth asking local builders or demolition contractors for old tiles, but there is a heavy demand for them and they are difficult to find. The answer for floor renovation, however, could lie literally beneath your feet, for you may find that all you need to do is take up the tiles and turn them over. The undersides of old tiles are often surprisingly well

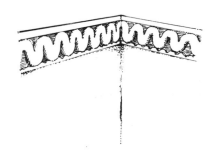

Ornamental plasterwork on cornices and covering was very much the vogue in mid-Victorian homes.

preserved and it is worth examining this possibility before opting for a complete modern replacement floor in tile or concrete.

Another approach where there are many broken or very badly worn tiles is to make a concrete floor in the centre of the room, which can be covered with a rug or small carpet, and surround it with whatever tiles can be saved.

Whenever a tile floor has to be relaid the opportunity should be taken to damp-proof, by excavating and putting in an under-layer of concrete incorporating a damp-proof membrane. Damp is of course often a major problem in timber floors at ground level, the particularly vulnerable areas being where the floorboards meet the walls. Regular inspection, including if necessary taking up damaged boards, is vital so that remedial action can be taken as quickly as possible. (Details of treatment and cure of rot and worm damage are given on p 81). To prevent rot it is essential to have the floorboards as well ventilated as possible and airbricks in the walls below floor level can help greatly.

People tend to worry more about the state of their upper floors, imagining that bed or bath are likely to come tumbling through to the floor below. In fact upper floors are less susceptible to damp than those near ground level, and as a general rule the older the floor the more secure it is likely to be, since larger quantities of good quality timber will have been used in its construction. The best first test of its soundness is simply to jump up and down on it a few times. If it gives rather too much and bounces back sluggishly, there may well be worm attack to the joists. If you cannot see these from below, then prise up a few boards to see what is going on. (You may have to remove the skirting board first.) Look carefully at joists and the undersides of the boards for signs of infestation: if all seems well, you can nail back the boards, but if there is any worm damage, the wisest course is to take up all the boards. Mark them with chalk so that they can be fitted back in the same position. If the infestation is not too bad it will just be a question of cutting away and replacing the odd areas of worm damage or rot, but joists showing a lot of damage should be replaced.

Where there is only a little infestation give it a good going-over with a wire brush. (See p 81 for identification of rot and worm damage.) Next apply a couple of coats of an all-purpose fungicide/insecticide/wood preservative, all over the joists and other timbers, and on the undersides of the floorboards. Replace the boards and nail into position, sweep clean and paint them over with a mixture of wood stain and preservative. The back of the skirting boards should be treated with preservative too before being nailed home.

If the floor is not badly damaged it may not be necessary to go to all that bother, but merely to cover the boards (after a good all-purpose preservative treatment) with a layer of dense chipboard, nailed or screwed down. This can have a remarkable strengthening effect for a comparatively small outlay.

If worm or rot damage is really bad, or if there are distinct structural problems then it is really best to call in an expert, who will know of sophisticated techniques for reinforcing floors. Some of these techniques are detailed in a pamphlet 'Strengthening Timber Floors', available from the Society for the Protection of Ancient Buildings.

Staircases

The staircase started life as a purely functional piece of household equipment, a rude and crude means of ascending and descending to and from the upper floors. It gradually became less cramped and inconvenient and it evolved through the magnificent joinery work of Elizabethan, Jacobean and Commonwealth staircases, and the soaring, curving splendour of Georgian stairs, to be the finest and most prominent interior architectural feature of the house. But then its importance declined again, function rather than form and style being the major requirement in Victorian and modern times.

As with most social changes, the grander houses set the fashion – whether for staircases, or fireplaces, doors and windows – and provided the inspiration for change and development on a smaller scale in lesser houses.

In the earliest houses, of course, there was no need for a staircase, most homes being single-storey affairs. Exceptions included the stone houses of King John's days where the living rooms were on the upper floor, generally reached by a straight flight of stone stairs on the outside, and the upper-floor Hall houses where access was again by external steps. There were also tower houses, with storage room at the base, living accommodation on the first floor, and bedrooms on second and, possibly, subsequent storeys. These would be connected by a spiral staircase, either built into the thickness of the walls or accommodated in its own small projecting turret.

The owner of the everyday early medieval house lived, slept and ate at ground level, with nothing between his floor and the roof over his head. As time progressed, part of the hall would be divided off into the rooms with more privacy, and their flat ceilings provided another area for accommodation above. This would usually be reached by a straight ladder resting against the partition wall, or later by a more elaborate but no less cramped and inconvenient 'companionway' – a series of treads and strings (the timber planks holding the treads) built into a shallow recess. One of the problems for the medieval carpenter was that he did not have the technique of making the staircase pass through the floor itself. So when enclosing his stairs he had to build a shallow cupboard to

In medieval times the domestic circular stone staircase was very much a smaller reflection of those built for castles of the age.

carry the treads and strings to support the ends of the two or three floor joists cut back to take the stairway. This form of staircase is seldom now to be seen, having been replaced by more sophisticated versions, although it does survive in the primitive 'croglofft' cottages of Wales and Ireland and, in more substantial form, in the straight-flight stone steps that were built into some of the better medieval houses.

An early 17th century framed newel staircase with straight flights and square landings. This style enabled the carpenter to show off his skills with carefully carved posts topped with elaborate finials.

As the hall house developed, with the addition of either one or two double-storeyed wings or with a complete upper floor covering the whole of the house area, more staircases were obviously needed, but narrow straight flights of cramped spirals were all that were on offer for centuries.

The spiral staircase was the everyday reflection of the stone spirals of medieval castles. Tight and steeply-stepped, it turned in a complete half circle and for this reason the stairways were often known as caracoles, from the French term *caracoler,* for a horse and rider to execute a turn to left or right. The steps would be made of stone, or from solid wooden planks slotted into the timber walls and radiating from a central mast-like pole or newel. The stairs might be built around the fireplace, the space between the chimney stack and wall being a very convenient one, or they might be tucked into some other internal corner. Alternatively, and particularly in stone-building areas, the stairway was contained in a semi-circular bulge projecting from the building, often in the angle where hall and two-storeyed wing met.

Staircases gradually became less cramped, a significant breakthrough in their development coming in the 16th century when the fireplace moved. From being built on the line of an outside wall, the chimney was moved to the middle of the house, and the staircase could conveniently curve around its massive stack. This innovation seems first to have occurred in the south-eastern counties of England in Elizabeth I's reign. And although it soon spread elsewhere in the country, it was by no means universal: in the Midlands, in Cambridgeshire and Huntingdonshire, for instance, the stack usually stood free and unencumbered by stairs.

By the end of the 16th century many of the larger houses had become three-storeyed, with not only a first floor but another above it, creating rooms in the roof space. Tight spirals or cramped straight flights were therefore even more inconvenient. One solution was to ascend each floor in three flights, with right-angled turns between them, so the stairs still described a 180 degree turn. The steps were made of stone or timber, arranged around a solid central core of stone or brick. Such staircases were easier to use than the tight spiral, but took up about three times the space of a winding stair. So in smaller houses a common arrangement was to have two instead of three flights, the second reversing the direction of the first at a half-landing. This configuration was known as 'dog-leg' stairs or 'a pair of stairs'.

To give more room for the larger staircase, a special wing or outshut was often built on the wall of the house. This was common feature in the south and east in the early 17th century and became widespread in the Midlands between 1650 and 1700. Another way of gaining more space was to build a storeyed porch at the front of the house, containing both entrance door and staircase, a style that was popular in the Lake District and a few other parts of the north.

The three-flight arrangement around a solid core gave little scope for display and decoration, so it soon developed into a grander staircase which gave more chance to the carpenter to show off his skills and the owner to impress his neighbours. This was the framed newel staircase, in which the central core is abolished and replaced by newel posts at the angles of each of the turns, creating an open well. Elaborate carving on the newels and balusters turned the staircases into works of art and, in a later development, into works of great joinery skill too. Here the newels were shortened to become separate posts at each landing, again carefully carved and often topped with beautifully-designed finials.

Balusters, the curving pillars supporting the rail were a product of the renaissance revival, emanating from Italy. The name itself derives from the Greek *balaustion,* the wild pomegranate flower, whose shape they were supposed to resemble. Early versions, however, were tubby imitations of the classical design and were often not turned but carved from planks of oak. Magnificent wooden staircases reached their zenith in Jacobean and Commonwealth times, with a variety of intricate designs and elaborate woodwork. By the end of the 17th century owners wanted to have a framed staircase rising impressively from the central hall. The fashion for the central fireplace and chimney stack, however, meant that there was not enough space for an imposing staircase – and so the chimney changed its position, back to the gable ends, to make way for the staircase.

As the 18th century progressed stairways became ever lighter and more graceful, with slimmer balusters in greater number. The Georgian house plan eliminated for ever the great chimney in the centre of the house. In the medium-size and larger dwellings the entrance door was centred on the house front and opened into a large hall filled with what had now become the most prominent interior architectural feature, the staircase. Later in this period the development of iron-smelting with coke meant the increasing use of ironwork in architecture and even more beautiful staircase designs in cast-iron with delicate sweeping curves. As the staircase was central and away from the windows, it needed its own source of light and another Georgian feature is the small turret capped with a glass cupola, lighting the staircase from above. More light also came from the glass fan above the door.

In smaller houses, however, there was no room for such magnificence and because of the lack of space the dog-leg or 'pair of stairs' design more often found favour, particularly in the terraced houses which had begun to make their appearance in the second half of the 18th century. The typical better-class terrace house had a front door opening into a narrowish hall (called a 'passage' in the north) with the dog-leg stairs ascending

The Georgian house plan had no need of a great chimney in the centre of the house, so opening up the entrance hall for a large and imposing staircase. As the 18th century progressed staircases became lighter and more graceful with slimmer balusters, some even made of delicate ironwork.

out of it to a half-landing and then back on themselves to reach the first floor. In many such houses a further boxed-in staircase led to the large attic room. Dog-leg stairs, or even a flight rising from the hall and making just one right-angled turn to the landing, were to become the norm right up to modern times. In the open-plan houses popular in the 1950s and 1960s, open tread staircases (that is with no risers) were often made a feature, but they were generally plain and simple compared with earlier splendours.

REPAIRS AND RENOVATIONS

It is most important that the stairs in an old house are kept in good condition, since worn and broken stairs can be dangerous and even deadly. Treads and risers, usually made of softwood, are particularly susceptible to rot and worm infestation and should therefore be inspected regularly, looking particularly for penetrating damp if the stairs run against an outside wall. Worm damage can be spotted easily if the undersides of the treads and risers are accessible, but often they are covered over, by lath and plaster for instance, so a more careful inspection of the upper surfaces is called for. (Details on the identification of rot and worm problems and their treatment are given on p 81.) To prevent rot it helps to have the space beneath the ground or basement floor staircase adequately ventilated, to keep the damp at bay.

Stairs are also subject to wear, and to mechanical instability, caused by shrinkage of the treads and risers or by settlement of the supporting structure. All this will almost certainly lead to creaks and in later stages could be downright dangerous. Look out for tell-tale gaps between surfaces which should fit snugly together. The adjustment of the staircase using wedges or tie rods should not be beyond the skills of the house owner, provided that the structure is not too complicated, but a skilled carpenter will be needed for the finer assemblies. For advice on how to 'do it yourself' there are plenty of house repair manuals available. The balusters and newels of staircases have often been killed by kindness, by layer upon layer of paint obscuring the fine carving work. If you can find the time all old paint should be stripped off and the wood either varnished or freshly painted. Handrails, particularly, were often made of mahogany, oak or another good hardwood, and covering them over with paint is a tragedy. Humbler pine balusters and handrails, too, can be pleasing features if left in the natural wood, even though this may not have been the original designer's intention.

Fireplaces and chimneys

There is no smoke without fire, we say, but the early house-dweller would know only too well that the converse is also true: there is not fire without smoke. A hearth in the home was essential, of course, for winter warmth – and year-round cooking – but while the fire might burn brightly and merrily, medieval houses must have been very draughty or very smoky, or an uncomfortable combination of both.

Matters would have been much improved by the Tudor and Elizabethan eras, with great fireplaces and solid chimney stacks taking over from the open hearth; and by Georgian and Regency times, helped by the replacement of wood by coal as a fuel, the fireplace had become not only reasonably efficient but also a focus of ornament and design in stylish rooms. The Victorian fireplace, too, was the dominant feature of the room – often over-bearing in its shape and structure.

The Romans had brought to Britain sophisticated house-warming systems, including central heating using hot air ducts, but most homes of ordinary people continued to use the traditional, smoky, sooty method: a large fire on a central hearth of stones. In Saxon and medieval Britain wood was in plentiful supply and once lit, the fire would be kept burning almost continuously. Slow-burning oak would be the fuel of preference, giving more heat for less smoke. To blaze merrily, though, a fire needs a good supply of air, and that came in through ill-fitting doors, windows and shutters, its icy blasts diverted but hardly halted by strategically placed screens.

The smoke was allowed to escape through a hole in the roof or often through triangular gaps left at the top of the gable ends, but such systems were far from efficient.

An early improvement was to fit the smoke-escape holes with louvres, which while encouraging the smoke outwards, kept the rain from coming in. In poorer houses the louvres would be simply made from wattle or from thatch, but in better-off homes, especially from the 13th century onwards, timber or pottery louvres, frequently well-decorated, were incorporated, often built into their own chimney-like structures.

The hall house was one of the principal architectural concepts in housebuilding; a form that existed, with modifications, right up to the 17th century. With the fire burning on its central hearth, use of the upper space in the hall was not practicable, for here the smoke gathered before filtering out through the roof. Later, however, one end of the hall would be partitioned off, or a double-storeyed wing or two would be added on to its central section. Such extra rooms would obviously be cold, being separated from the main hearth, so smaller fireplaces were often put in the wall to heat them. The word chimney originally meant fireplace, originating from the Latin *caminata* , a room with a fireplace, which itself derived from the Greek *kaminor* , oven.

Those who lived in tower houses, or upper floor hall houses would have had wall fireplaces as a matter of course, augmented sometimes by a central brazier. In the grand houses, too, particularly those of a semi-fortified nature, wall fireplaces were a common feature.

Wall fireplaces

The first major improvement in the hall house was to move the principal fireplace from its central hearth to a side wall, a move that usually came in the 15th century. This then allowed the whole of the upper part of the Hall to be floored over, providing two storeys. The smoke from the big wall fireplace was collected in a large, funnel-shaped hood – usually made of timber with thick daub, or in some areas of stone – which might push out up to 5 ft into the room. This hood extended into the second-storey room, where it provided much-needed radiant heat, before ending just below the louvred smoke exits. In some areas platforms were built on either side of the hood, for storage, for seats or even for beds – the cosiest in the house.

Alternatively, the chimney stack was built outside the line of the hall, in many ways a better alternative since it helped to keep the hot gases and sparks away from the inflammable thatch. Usually, of course, it was best to put the chimney on the gable end, where it was well clear of the thatch, but in some house designs, such as the hall with two end wings, this was impracticable, so the chimney would be on a side wall (normally the back one). It was easier to build a chimney here since it did not have to extend so high, but it created problems because the joint between the chimney and roof would collect rain water and be liable to penetrating damp. So the area was often protected by a small pitched roof, set at a right angle to the main roof.

Chimneys were being built in increasing numbers in the 15th century, and most houses had a chimney stack of some kind by the end of the 16th century. But they were not universal, perhaps due to the difficulty in finding skilled craftsmen to build them. A stone chimney required a mason's skills and he would be expensive and difficult to inveigle away

A major innovation in the medieval hall house was the re-siting of the central hearth to a side wall where the smoke was channelled up a large hood. It became common by the 15th century.

from the castle, grand houses and monastery where he found most of his employment. So even in the 16th century, and particularly in south-eastern England, some houses still had a central, one-storey hall with a fire burning in an open hearth and its smoke escaping, slowly, out of a hole in the roof. But the dissolution of the monasteries released large numbers of masons from their ecclesiastic labours and helped to usher in the great era of fireplace and chimney building in late Tudor and Elizabethan times.

TUDOR AND ELIZABETHAN FIREPLACES

We have seen how the medieval fireplace extended deep into the room with a wide hearth and a canopy over to take away the smoke. In Tudor times a much more deeply recessed fireplace with a thick external chimney stack became the normal pattern. So much chimney building went on in the 16th century that it became known as 'The Age of Chimneys' and in 1577 an observer wrote of 'the multitude of chimneys lately erected'.

As well as stone, brick was increasingly used for the chimney stack, and the fireplace surround was a fresh ground for the craftsman to carve and decorate. The opening was sometimes properly arched, although more often the lintel was merely carved in an arch shape (usually four-centred). At the corners the spandrels could be decorated with some heraldic design.

153

The central stack

The major innovation, however came in around the beginning of the 17th century with the introduction of the central or axial chimney stack which rapidly became popular.

This era also saw the burgeoning of a prosperous middle-class, not only of merchants but of affluent farmers looking for better housing than that enjoyed (or endured) by their forefathers. Some might have an axial stack built into their existing houses; others wanted new houses and a mini-industry grew up to meet that demand.

The central chimney was the most expensive feature of the new style houses. It was a really solid structure, built of stone or brick according to the area, and was the first thing to be put up on site. It provided the core of the house, a prop for the whole building (and, incidentally it made it possible to economise as wood became scarcer, since shorter lengths of timber could now be used). In the case of fire, unfortunately all too common in the 17th century, the chimney might be all that was left standing and would form the basis for rebuilding.

The standardised Elizabethan and Jacobean farmhouse was rectangular in shape, the chimney stack dividing it internally into two portions, one somewhat smaller than the other. In plan the chimney stack was in the shape of an H, two fireplaces back to back opening into kitchen and parlour. The central stack also provided an ideal place around which to build the staircase.

From the ground floor the wide stack continued upwards, opening into two more fireplaces in the chambers above, and out into the roof, where it was finished off in a cluster of four chimneys. Here beautiful patterns and decorations often made the chimney the house's crowning glory: so much so that it is no exaggeration to suggest that chimney tops were one of england's greatest contributions to the architecture of the Renaissance period.

A point about dating here. Beautiful brick chimneys were a major feature of Tudor buildings of grand houses (Hampton Court is a classic example), and while those who could afford it quickly aped their betters, fine chimneys in everyday houses are generally of a later period, from the 17th century on.

Axial chimneys were not only built in new houses, but put into existing ones, and their position depended on the size and shape of the house. The fireplace that had become a splendid feature in the great houses and palaces of Tudor and Elizabethan England often reflected that charming half-assimilated renaissance work that is to be found in other architectural detail of the period, where classical features are intermingled with earlier design and styling. Above the carved over-mantel, for instance, there would often be a series of arched recesses. Another design replaced the over-mantel with a large moulded panel, sometimes orna- mented, but often with very clean and simple lines.

The farm and cottage fireplace

In the less imposing homes, and in farmhouses, the fireplace now occupied the pride of place, but while it was large in scale it was much simpler in design. The fireplace surround might be dressed in stone or merely have a solid oak beam, called a bressumer, across the top of the opening, shaped to imitate the stone prototype and supported on pillars of brick or stone. In its simplest form the Elizabethan fireplace showed little or no decoration, the massive lintel being a straight oak beam. In the east and south-east of England, where brick-building techniques were highly developed, the fireplace surround would be framed entirely in moulded bricks. there were often recesses in the sides of the bigger fireplaces, with shelves for storage, (especially to keep the salt dry), or with seats, possibly with built-in arm rests. These are cosy *inglenooks* – the work ingle coming from the Gaelic *aingael,* meaning fire or light. The big fireplace was still used for cooking as well as warmth, so there would spits and pots and pans hanging about it, and behind the chimney breast a large iron bar ran across the fire, from which were hung sides of bacon or ham for smoking.

One of the troubles with both brick and stone is that they are damaged by heat, so they were protected by ornamental plates or firebacks, which began to appear towards the end of the 16th century, turned out in quantity particularly by the iron foundries in Sussex. Also in the late 17th century ovens were built into the thick back of the fireplace and closed with a stout cast iron door. They were heated at night – filled with embers from the fire, which were raked out in the morning for bread and pies to be popped in.

Among the other items of fireplace furniture were firedogs, metal supports to stop the large logs from rolling out into the room. Medieval in origin, firedogs were an essential part of the hearth until coal replaced wood as the common fuel.

In 1662, to provide more income for his Exchequer and to help pay for the army, Charles II introduced a Hearth Tax, of two shillings per year for every fireplace, hearth and stove in all but the smallest cottages. It is doubtful whether all of the tax reached the royal coffers, for its collection was put out to freelance agents who were less than scrupulous in their returns. Some agents would mark the main bressumer to show that the house was registered for hearth tax, and these marks can still sometimes be seen. In fact if you can find the listing of the house in the local tax returns for the period you can work out whether the house has been enlarged later by comparing the number of hearths then and now. The tax, always unpopular, was repealed at the end of the 17th century.

Regional fireplace fashions

As always there are many regional variations from these basic designs. In the stone-bearing regions of Devon and Cornwall, for instance, the usual position of a chimney stack in houses built of stone or cob was at the front of the house. It is not as convenient as the axial stack, since its fireplaces only heat two rooms, one on each floor (the hall and the chamber above it). Its position was probably motivated by pride: by putting a new-fangled chimney stack at the front, the owner showed that he was a man of some substance. The chimney was often built in contrasting materials – limestone and sandstone, for example, or in limestone with a chequerwork of flint and stone – further to emphasize its importance.

In the stone-building areas of the Cotswolds, too, the axial stack never became popular and in the Lake District the difficulties of building squared-off corners using undressed stone led to the use of circular chimney stacks.

The axial stack was not necessarily the only chimney in the house, especially in the larger farmhouses in the south and east of England. Often they would have a second parlour (a forerunner of the dining-room) attached to the end of the living room/kitchen, in addition to the parlour at the other side of the central stack. This extra room needed heating too and a small additional fireplace would be built at the gable end.

LATE 17TH CENTURY TO PRESENT DAY

In Tudor, Elizabethan and Jacobean times, each fire had its own chimney top, with individual shafts beautifully decorated, but by the late 17th century the whole stack was being transformed into a solid structure, either square or cruciform in plan, with the flues concealed within it. We can see in these chimneys echoes of classical shapes and patterns, with projecting courses of bricks imitating classical entabulature. In this period staircases became the most prominent internal feature of the house and the demand for a grand, central staircase relegated the fireplace again to the edges of the house rather than the middle. As with most innova-

Georgian architects took less interest in the construction of efficient chimneys but devoted their talents to beautifying the fireplaces they served. They reflected the classical design and proportions, embellished often with shouldered decorated architraves supporting the overmantel.

tions this started with larger houses but it had spread to all types of everyday house by the mid-18th century. In some ways it was a retrogressive step since the central stack helped warm the whole house, but it was permanent; never again was the fireplace to assume a dominating central position in the ordinary home.

In the double-pile house fireplaces were usually built into the end walls, although in eastern England especially it was not uncommon to place them back-to-back on a partition wall.

The Georgian architect faced something of a problem in designing fireplaces and chimney stacks: his buildings followed classical lines, but there were, of course, no classical models of fireplaces for him to follow. As John Woodforde write in *Georgian Houses for All* : 'Palladio's chimneys had been just tubes put almost anywhere (but unobtrusively) and Georgian builders as though following him in this, took far less interest in the construction of chimneys than their predecessors. But whatever the inadequacy of some Georgian chimney stacks, leading to present-day dampness in bedroom ceilings, much attention was devoted to beautifying the fireplaces they served.' The classical allusions can be seen everywhere in Georgian fireplaces and chimneypieces. More often than not the sides of the fireplace were mock columns but even if they were not, their proportions echoed the classical modes, with sections corresponding to base, shaft and capital. the lintel and chimney breast above were modelled on classical entabulature.

In large houses, of course, there had been some signs of classical influence as early as the late 16th and early 17th century, but in Wren's time (the late 17th century) the form that found favour was a straightforward surround with a plain bulging moulding, set into oak panelling. This was followed by a vogue for fireplace surrounds with a shouldered architrave to which might be added decorative scrolls and, to break the long line of the overmantel, a central keystone or tablet.

In the middle Georgian period the typical fireplace had its pilasters, or uprights, surmounted by curved ornamental brackets (consoles) which

A characteristic of the Victorian fireplace was to surround the iron grate with decorative tiles, especially in the best parlour.

158

supported the mantel. A broad mantelshelf was not typical of this period, although it might be added later. As with the other features of the house, the Georgian architect paid great attention to detail in the fireplaces, and precise instructions as to proportions and decorations were laid down in the specifications and the builders' manual.

The chimney breast in ordinary houses was at first fairly plain with perhaps just one large panel with decorated edges, where a picture could be hung or a mirror fitted. Another popular style was to have three panels, two narrow ones at the sides and a large central one.

The full flowering of Georgian style came in late 18th century fireplaces, notably in the design of Robert Adam. In the fireplaces of the great houses neo-classicism was rife, richly-draped female figures supporting the mantelshelf, which had now become fairly broad. The less extravagant fireplaces of the everyday house did not aspire to statuary, but were nonetheless well-decorated and ornamented by mouldings, which were mass-produced in a variety of styles by specialist workshops. The most characteristic feature of Adam-style fireplaces was the central plaque, moulded in the most delicate curving designs.

Marble was the material of choice for early Georgian fireplaces and even those in small houses had marble hearths and surrounds. Later, however, painted wood took over, carved in imitation of the stone prototypes, with added mouldings.

Coal replaces wood

One of the reasons why fireplaces could now be so elegant in design and delicate in ornamentation was that they suffered less damage in everyday use, because coal was replacing wood as the common fuel. It had begun to come into domestic use towards the end of Tudor times, being brought from the Northumberland coalfields to London and the east coast towns by boat. Because coal was easier to handle than logs and needed less vigorous poking and stoking, the surround was less liable to be knocked about. And since it is slower-burning, both the fireplace opening and the chimney flue could be narrower. In the old wide chimneys, cleaning was not too great a problem – a man could get a fair way up and scratch off the soot with a broom of holly leaves. But in the narrower flues, only small boys could squeeze up and generations of tiny chimneysweeps were employed to clean them, a horrifying trade. Some small relief, however, was given to these unfortunate boys by an Act of Parliament in 1840 which set minimum requirements for the width of the flues.

Early grates to hold the coal were tall affairs, placed fairly high in the fireplace opening, with fronts of heavy bowed bars. In the bedrooms and the lesser public rooms, the grate with a hob on the side appeared, the most popular style being the duck's next grate, the upper semi-circle of bars being supported on a semi-circular arch. Such grates could be in fairly plain cast-iron or in decorated relief echoing the classical details of the principal fireplace.

Chimney pots were most uncommon before the 18th century, although they had been occasionally used as early as the 13th century. It was said that they were introduced to provide a better draught, but they in fact add little to the chimney's efficiency that cannot be achieved by building the stack and flue properly. They were probably first used as a device for adding height to the chimney stacks that protruded from houses with hipped roofs. Such stacks would be unsupported from the level of the eaves upwards and in order to gain the height necessary to avoid down-draughts, a light chimney pot would be added. They may also have been needed to help improve the up-draught in house where there were many fireplaces and a tortuous system of flues, full of curves and angles. Whatever the reason for their introduction, they became very popular in the late 18th century and had become standard additions to the chimney stack in Victorian times. They look somewhat incongruous excrescences on the classical outline of the Georgian house and it is quite common to remove them in renovation today. (An interesting variation on the chimney pot is a pair of inclined slates resting on the top of the stack, seen particularly in areas like the Lake District. Although these may appear to be ancient, most of them are 19th century.)

In the 19th century we first see the development of the Georgian style into Regency, characterised by lighter designs, and then the move into the Victorian age with its variety of styles and revivals, notably the gothic, which was reflected in fireplaces as everywhere else inside and outside the house. Many a living room fireplace became florid, fussy and overblown, with solidly carved or turned woodwork, especially in the overmantles. One characteristic style of the Victorian period was to surround the iron grate with decorative tiles; after a long period out of fashion, these fireplaces are now often preserved, in recognition of a certain period charm.

In the 19th century kitchen a wide fireplace was still needed to accommodate all the paraphernalia of cooking: the pots and pans and spits and kettles (swung on chains over the open fire). The oven was usually built into the wall at the side of the fireplace and heated independently. By the end of the century, however, the kitchen 'range' was coming in, with a built-in oven and a boiler for heating water. Ranges certainly made cooking easier, and became almost universal in the 19th century, but they did take a lot of fuel to keep the pots boiling, the bread baking and the water bubbling. Ultimately the side boiler of the kitchen range gave way to a back boiler to heat the water, with taps directly to the kitchen sink, and to free-standing gas and electric cookers with their hot plates and ovens.

REPAIRS AND RENOVATIONS

In a house built before the 18th century the original fireplaces will probably have been since drastically altered – converted from wood to coal-burning, for instance, or filled with a Victorian or modern grate and surround. The original fireplace, even perhaps with an inglenook, may still be there, hidden behind the 'improvements' and it can be exposed to its former glory with a little time and effort.

The first job is to locate the original fireplace lintel or bressumer, which will most likely be somewhere above the top of the replacement fireplace. In many conversions to coal-burning the lintel was left exposed, but equally in many others it was completely plastered over. If there are no signs of it (look for the outline of its shape beneath wall paint or paper), then the only thing to do is to dig for it, probing carefully into the plaster with chisels and scrapers. Once found, and the surrounding plaster scraped away, the lintel's condition should be carefully examined. If it is not perfectly sound, it may need to be replaced by a similar baulk of timber. This is a job probably best left to a builder.

More often than not the solid oak beam will be whole and sound, and the laborious and dusty task of removing the newer fireplace can begin. There may even be two fireplaces of earlier dates behind the modern facade, but with luck the brickwork of the original cavity will soon be cleared. All the mess and rubble should be cleared away and the bricks of the supporting plinths and the side of the fireplace should be cleaned thoroughly by wirebrushing. Nothing looks better in an old house than a cheery wood fire burning in a large original fireplace, but it has to be admitted that this is a far from efficient means of heating, using considerable amounts of fuel, sending much of the heat up the chimney and dragging in icy draughts of cold air across the room. There are alternatives. The draughts can be cut down by taking in air through an airbrick or two put into the wall of an outside chimney, or by an under-floor conduit from the outside, ending in a grille at or near the hearth. Such devices also help invigorate the flow of smoke up the chimney so that it does not billow out into the room.

c) 15th century turret

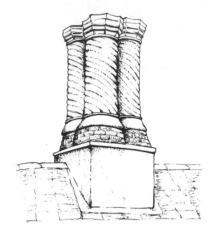

d) 16th century ornate Tudor

e) 17th century square brick

f) 18th century square chimney on Dutch gable

Smoking problems

Smoking can be a problem in a newly opened-up chimney, but as well as checking that it is reasonably clean and free from obstructions, other action can be taken to overcome it. The fire can be raised higher in the fireplace opening, either by putting bricks in the base of the firebasket, or by raising the basket itself, supporting its feet on bricks. Alternatively a hood to trap and carry off the smoke can be inserted into the fireplace opening.

Using a firebasket, however, does not solve the problem of fuel consumption and another alternative is to instal a cast-iron wood-burning stove. These now come in a variety of attractive styles and are increasingly popular in country districts. With them, at least, the hearth and fireplace surround can be seen as they originally were. But perhaps the best answer is to keep the open fire for show and put in discreet central heating for warmth and comfort. If you decide not to use the fireplace but merely have it as an interesting feature of the room the chimney should be blocked off to prevent heat loss.

For houses built in the 18th and 19th centuries, with coal-burning grates, smoking should not be much of a problem, for by that time many experts had bent their minds to produce the ideal design.

The appearance of many an 18th and 19th century room has been spoiled by replacing the original grates and surrounds with modern fitted fireplaces. When renovating such a house you may again, as with older houses, like to consider reversing the process: out with the new and back with the old.

Repairing chimneys

The exposed chimney stack is the part most vulnerable to damage and decay. Assaulted on the outside by the weather, it is attacked from within by acid residues in the smoke, which eat into the bricks and mortar.

The weather attacks the chimney structure on two fronts. On the side facing the prevailing wind, driving rain weakens and wears away at the joints between the bricks. The other side away from the wind dries out only slowly, and when the water in and around it freezes and expands in the winter, tensions are set up which tend to make the chimney lean and, ultimately, topple. Chimneys should be examined whenever possible, during other roof work for instance, and repaired as necessary. At the same time the damp-excluding layer where chimney stack meets roof should be checked and renovated.

If damage extends only to the mortar, then re-pointing is all that is required, trowelling fresh mortar into the cracks after they have been carefully raked out. The mortar should be slightly recessed, never proud, and finished off with a brush to bring the harder aggregate in it to the surface. If the bricks (or stones) themselves are badly worn, then more extensive work needs to be done, although it is generally accepted that a chimney will remain sound if re-pointed, even if as much as a quarter of the bricks' thickness has been worn away.

For more serious decay, and especially if there are a fair number of cracked or eroded bricks, the only solution is to take down and rebuild the top of the stack, using as many of the original bricks as possible. Old bricks to plug the gaps can probably be found at local builders or demolition contractors. This might prove an opportune time to rebuild the stack in a style more in keeping with the house, replacing a later plain stack with an earlier, perhaps more elaborate, design. Your local authority's Architect's Department should be able to help with details of local traditions.

Before going to the trouble and expense of demolishing and rebuilding, however, and particularly if the stack is an ornate one, consider the possibility of *in situ* repairs. There are a number of clever techniques for strengthening stacks from the inside, using reinforced concrete.

Chimney pots, made of baked clay, are less weather-resistant than the main stack and will wear or crack more quickly. The squared pots of white clay which became popular in the Georgian and Regency period are difficult to replace, although they could be made up to original designs by a local pottery. Fractured pots with some life left in them can be strengthened by binding with copper or stainless steel wire and coating with stone paint, but if the damage is too great, simply removing them may be the best answer. Many chimney pots are later additions to old property and not an integral part of the original design. Another alternative is to swap the damaged pots in prominent positions with sounder ones from less conspicuous places. Chimney stacks which are no longer used should be capped off to stop the rain coming in, but again some ventilation is needed to prevent the build-up of damp in the flue.

4

HOW TO DATE
A HOUSE

When Was it Built?

INTRODUCTION

The aim of this section of the book is to provide a simple technique for identifying and dating with a fair degree of accuracy the old houses in our towns and villages and in the countryside. By answering a few straightforward questions about the houses you are looking at, you will be able to 'home in' on their type, style and date.

You will, however, be judging by external appearance and it is entirely possible and indeed, quite likely that the face a house shows to the world will be much younger than the bones beneath. Many old houses had new facades imposed upon them and had their windows, doors and decorative features altered as owners sought to modernise their properties and keep up with prevailing fashions. It is often possible to find out more about the original building by looking at the sides and back of a house, which have been altered little, and at such basic attributes as the depth of the house, the height of the storeys and the pitch of the roof.

For the church and the grand country house, style and decorative features enable experts to date building and re-building with great accuracy (to say nothing of the help they receive from documentary evidence, so often conspicuously lacking for the smaller house.) For the everyday house, such precise dating is not so easy, because the timing of the introduction of new formats and features and of their abandonment varies greatly, due to a number of factors.

First, there is geographical location. As a general rule new ideas were introduced in the south-east of England and spread slowly northwards and westwards. It could be many, many decades before a new style penetrated to the more remote areas, by which time it could well have been superseded in its place of origin. There are, however, many exceptions to the general geographical rule, one of the most striking being East Anglia which was innovative and influential in the Middle

Ages, but later declined when the prosperous wool trade of the area ended.

Secondly, the size or status of a building often determined the use of novel features; they occur first in larger houses and only later are used in smaller ones, in cottages and in farm buildings. In addition, more conservative local builders continued to use older styles and features many years after more progressive ones had moved on to the new, so buildings in different styles, even in the same area, may date from the same period.

Nonetheless, most of us with a passing interest in old houses do not normally want to date them with the precision of an expert. We are content with a fair idea of their age and style. Working your way through this section will enable you to achieve just that.

First, to get a 'feel' for the house in front of you, ask a few basic questions . . .

SOME BASIC QUESTIONS

1. Where is it?

In towns and villages, older houses tend to be in the centre, near the church and marketplace. Outer suburbs tend to be a later development, although they sometimes absorb older villages. Street names, e.g. George Street, Waterloo Place, Sebastopol Villas can help, too. Look out for Georgian rectories, Victorian villas.

Farmhouses in the countryside might be Tudor but often are Queen Anne or Georgian following enclosures of 18th century.

2. How tall are the storeys?

The general rule is the older the house, the lower the storeys. Jettying (protruding upper storeys) appears in 15th century, but less common by mid-16th. It is rare after end of 16th, especially in south-east, though it may continue elsewhere, particularly in towns, into early 17th.

In 18th and 19th centuries it was not common for the front and back walls to be raised and the roof flattened, giving more upper floor headroom. Look for tell-tale signs of new work, especially at the gable ends. Sometimes only the front was raised and rear of the roof retains its original steeper pitch.

3. How deep is the house?

Most smaller houses were only one room deep until the 18th century. Then two room deep (double pile) plan became popular. Earlier double pile may have M-shaped roof. Later the roof spans the whole depth. Look for later additions to earlier shallower houses.

4. How steep is the roof?

Up to 15th century, most smaller houses were thatched, except where thin local stone or slate was available. Thatched roofs would be steeply pitched (45 to 55 degrees, even steeper if long-straw used) to allow rainwater to flow off. Stone, slate, pantile roofs have shallower pitches. Tiles or slates may replace thatch on older steeper roofs. Look for telltale signs of an original thicker covering around chimney stacks and inside gables.

5. Is the main elevation symmetrical?

Symmetrical facade suggests late 17th century and beyond. May be remodelling. Check chimney stacks: they are difficult to re-site, so asymmetry suggests a new facade.

Answers to these questions will have provided some basic clues to the age of the house. For more precise identification we need to look at the materials used and at some of the finer details.

WHAT IS IT BUILT OF?

1. Is it built of timber?

Timber was the commonest material for everyday houses from medieval times, except in those areas where local stone was easily accessible. Few ordinary timber houses built before the 15th century survive, and these are usually homes of the better-off farmers, yeomen and merchants.

The earliest houses have large timber frames, strengthened with various braces, but from the mid-15th century in the north and west, and the late 16th elsewhere, smaller panels took over. Close vertical studding was popular, in the south-east especially, from the 16th century.

The shortage of good timber in the 17th century led to use of lighter and rougher timbers, covered with rendering, weatherboarding or tiles. Fire hazards and legislation meant the virtual end of timber-frame buildings from the late 18th century onwards.

168

Problems with dating timber houses come from the ease of alteration and from the fact that old timbers can easily be re-used – and frequently were, as good timber became scarce in the 17th century. Also watch out for 'fakes' where an old 'feel' is deliberately created using ancient timbers, which may have no structural function.

For further details turn to pages 172 to 175.

2. Is is built of stone?

Some notable examples of stone houses from the 12th century onwards still remain, such as the town houses of rich merchants or stone-built country hall houses. In areas where workable stone was readily available there has been a long tradition of stone building, even for smaller houses, although elsewhere they were uncommon until the 16th and 17th centuries.

By the 17th century, good quality small stone houses were being built in the Cotswolds and in other areas such as the south-west, although they were rare in the poorer areas of the north until the mid-17th century.

Flints and cobbles were also used as walling material, usually strengthened with stonework and, later, with brick.

Building techniques varied widely, according to the nature of the material, although generally the bigger stones were laid at the base and better quality stones were used for the quoins and around windows and doors. Rougher stone was used elsewhere and then frequently covered with limewash (often removed in the 19th century when there was a fashion for bare stone) or disguised with rendering.

Ashlar, a fine quality stone cut into rectangular blocks, was typical of high-quality Georgian building, although again cheaper, rougher-hewn stone was frequently used and rendered over. The 19th century saw the last period of widespread stone use before cheap transport made brick universally available.

Dating of smaller stone houses can be difficult, because the same building methods were used for centuries, and in general more attention needs to be paid to architectural features than to the building techniques themselves.

For more details, turn to pages 176 to 177.

3. Is it built of brick?

Bricks were little used in everyday houses before the 15th century, but the great rebuilding of the 16th and 17th centuries saw their increasingly widespread use. They were used first in the south and east and spread gradually throughout the country, first in better-class houses (replacing timber-framing and clay walls) and later in smaller ones.

By the late 17th century small brick houses were common and brick use was widespread in the 18th. Many timber and clay houses were refaced with brick in this period. Bricks were also used to replace wattle and daub panel in-filling.

Brick taxes (introduced in 1784 and finally abolished in 1850) encouraged production of larger bricks and the use of weatherboarding and imitation bricks, but mass production and cheap transport made bricks the universal construction material in the 19th century.

Early-hand made bricks were irregular in size and required more mortar in the joints. 19th century machine-made bricks were more regular and joints could be thinner.

Clues for the dating of brick buildings can also come from the colour of the bricks and from the patterns (bonds) in which they are laid. For more details turn to pages 178 to 179.

4. Is it made of clay or rendered over?

Clay was used as a walling material from the earliest times up to the 18th and 19th centuries. Cob, a mixture of clay and straw built up in layers, is typical of Devon, but similar techniques were used in the Midlands, Wales and the North-west. In East Anglia, clay lumps or bats were used: the clay/straw mixture being moulded into large oblong blocks. By the 19th century many clay-walled houses were re-faced with brick.

From the 18th century onwards, as good building timber became scarcer, wooden-frame houses were more often than not completely rendered over. There is a modern tendency to expose these timbers, but they were never meant to be seen.

If the house walls are less than a foot thick, there is probably a timber frame beneath; thicker walls, tapering from the base, and rounded corners indicate a clay construction. The windows also tend to be smaller. Many clay buildings are fairly recent, from the late 18th or early 19th centuries when there was a demand for cheap construction.

Dating clay houses can be difficult and the best clues come from architectural features, but the material used for the base of the wall may help: stone or flint was used earlier, brick later.

The rendering of timber-frame houses became popular in the 16th and 17th centuries (even in good quality housing in East anglia) with lime plaster laid on laths. While often plain (and white- or colour-washed), the plaster could be inscribed or moulded into intricate designs, known as pargetting. This can be seen from the late 16th century and was at its height in the late 17th and early 18th, but plain plastering was in vogue again in the mid-18th century. Pargetting enjoyed another comeback in the late 19th century.

Stucco, a cement-like plaster, was widely used by Georgian and early Victorian builders, especially in towns.

For more details turn to pages 180 to 181.

Timber-Framed Houses: what to look out for

Large panel framing. 14th/15th to 16th century.
    The earliest form of framing, found in all areas by mid-15th century. Only generally found in less important houses after beginning of 16th century; uncommon after mid-16th.

Plain large panel: 14th and 15th centuries.

Arch-bracing: 14th century onwards, common in Midlands.

Tension-bracing: 15th century onwards, popular in the south-east.

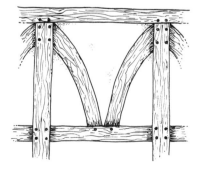

Smaller panel framing: 15th/16th to 17th century.

Seen in larger houses in the north and west from mid- 15th century. Much later in other areas and generally in smaller houses. Widespread in smaller houses by late 16th and in 17th centuries.

Plain small framing: mid-15th century onwards. Note small angle-brace.

Close studding: Late 15th to 17th century.

Most popular in the south-east and often associated with jettying. Panel members are same thickness as studs. They become more widely spaced as time went on. A middle rod may sometimes be seen in most areas except the north-east. Note: small framing and close studding use a lot of timber so large panels are frequently used at back or sides of house.

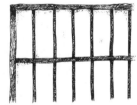

Close-studding: Late 15th century onwards.

Rough-timbered light framing: 17th to 19th century.

Seen from the 17th century onwards as good timber becomes scarce. Generally plastered, weatherboarded or tiled over and not intended to be seen (although sometimes exposed in restoration.) the plaster is sometimes moulded and decorated, especially in East Anglia. (See Rendering: pargetting) Timber frame building dying out by 19th century.

Rough timber, light framing, seen from the 17th century onwards.

173

Jettying: 15th to early 17th century.

Seen in the 15th century Wealden houses and is common in Tudor town houses. It began to die out by mid–16th century and became rare after the end of it in rural areas, especially the south-east. It continued in towns elsewhere into the early 17th century.

Timber-frame in-filling.

The earliest in-filling was wattle and daub, finished with limewash which sometimes continued over timbers. Timbers were generally not darkened, except in the north and west, especially in later ornamental work. (Blackening timbers developed in 19th century.) By the 16th century in the south and east, brick comes in, sometimes in a herring-bone pattern. Brick in-fill gradually spreads to other areas.

Typical examples of timber-framed house styles.

Cruck house: 14th to 18th century. See text page 13 for details.

174

Wealden house: 15th and 16th century.
See text page 16 for details.

Jettied house: 15th to early 17th century.
See text page 22 for details.

For further clues on dating, turn to Architectural Details, pp 182 to 185.

Stone-Built Houses: what to look out for.

Stone-building techniques: can all be used in different periods, check architectural details for dating.

Random rubble.

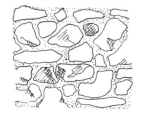

Coursed random rubble with larger, more regular stone quoins.

Flint with brick lacing course and quoins.

Fine ashlar masonry, typical of Georgian period. (Watch for rendered imitations.)

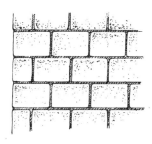

Typical examples of stone-built houses.

Rubble stone long house: 16th to 18th centuries. See text page 61 for details.

Cotswold stone house: 17th to 19th centuries. See text page 58 for details.

Georgian ashlar house: 18th century. See text page 31 for details.

For further clues on dating, turn to Architectural Details, pp 182 to 185.

Brick-Built Houses: what to look out for.

Brick sizes
Early bricks of around 14th and 15th centuries are about 2 inches high and 12 by 6 inches across. Brick thickness was fixed in 1571 at 2¼ inches high and 9 by 4½ across. These were called Statute bricks. Thick bricks, during Brick Tax period (late 18th to mid-19th centuries) are 3 inches high and more. Modern bricks are usually 2½ inches high. (more in the north.)

Brick colours
Red brick was popular in the 16th, 17th and early 18th centuries. Grey and brown was increasingly used in the 18th, with red brick dressings at quoins, door and window openings. By the late 18th century red was considered too bright: grey, yellow (London 'stock') and East Anglian 'whites' (pale grey) were widely used. By the late 19th century 'stock' acquired working class image, red made a comeback in better class houses.

Brick patterns (bonds)

English bond, typical of 16th and 17th centuries.

Flemish bond: common in 17th century, largely replaces English bond by early 18th.

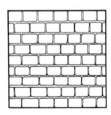

Header bond: popular in the 18th century.

Stretcher bond: generally seen in modern cavity walling.

Typical examples of brick-built house styles.

Tudor brick house: 15th and 16th centuries. See text pages 22 for details.

Queen Anne House: late 17th, early 18th centuries. See text page 28 for details.

Victorian terrace house: 19th century. See text page 42 for details.

For further clues on dating, turn to Architectural Details pp 182 to 185.

Rendered Houses: what to look out for.

Plaster laid on horizontal laths.

Pargetting: generally late 16th to middle 18th century.

Typical examples of clay-built or rendered houses.

Cob cottage, typical of Devon: medieval to 19th century. See text page 22 for details.

Rendered timber house with pargetting, late 16th to middle 18th century. See text page 55 for details.

Georgian stucco: late 18th, early 19th century. See text page 35 for details.

For further clues on dating, turn to Architectural Details pp 182 to 185.

Architectural Details

Architectural details like the shape, size and style of windows and doors, and their surrounds, can also give further clues to the dating of the house. But it is important to remember that such features may well have been altered or replaced over the years and their evidence must be weighed with other signs, like the shape of the house and the materials used in its construction.

The Windows.

Early windows tended to be long and low. In the smaller Medieval and early Tudor houses, they were usually unglazed and had internal shutters. The window space was divided by upright timber (or stone) mullions. The design of these mullions changed over the years and can give clues to dating. By the mid-16th century, glazing was more widespread and the mullions were adapted accordingly. By the late 16th and early 17th centuries side-hung casements in wood or iron had become more common and in the 18th century such windows often replaced the old mullioned ones in the smaller house and cottage.

By the 17th century as the influence of classical designs spread to everyday houses, windows in the better ones became taller and narrower, often only two lights wide and divided with a horizontal transom as well as a vertical mullion. The diamond pattern of the leaded lights gave way to a rectangular one. Brick houses of the 17th and early 18th centuries often had contrasting window surrounds and exaggerated keystones.

Sash windows came in during the late 17th and early 18th centuries. Early sash frames were flush with the wall but, because of the fire hazard, London Building Acts in 1707 and 1709 required them to be set back four inches. This change gradually spread to most of the rest of the country. A 1774 Act also required the frames to be recessed behind reveals, so little of frame is visible from the outside. Glazing bars became lighter as time progressed and could be very thin indeed by the 19th century.

Window taxes from 1695 to the end of the 18th century explain why some windows are blocked up, but 'blind' windows were often deliberately inserted in 18th century designs to obtain symmetry.

By the 19th century larger panes of glass were available and glazing bars could be omitted or removed (which often spoiled the appearance of older windows.)

Window shapes:

A long, low mullioned medieval/ early Tudor window.

A Georgian sash window, showing classical influence.

The medieval influence was strong in the Gothic revival of the 19th century.

For more information on windows see pp 111 pp 122

The doors

Medieval and Tudor doors tended to be pointed, but became flatter as time progressed. At first (in the 14th and 15th centuries) the two-centred arch was popular; the four-centred arch appeared in the 15th century and continued until the 17th, becoming flatter; other variations included the ogee and the shouldered arch.

The vertical plank doors were more often than not hung directly on to the wall, with a metal strap slotting on to a vertical pin. If there was a door frame it would be heavily-timbered.

By the end of the 17th century, the classical influence was becoming apparent even in smaller houses, and square-headed doorways became more and more common. Flat door hoods supported by console brackets characterised early 18th century doors while the latter part of the century saw the development of the classical pediment (with ornate variations) above moulded pilasters. Lighter panelled doors were common by the 18th century and the lighter doors could be hung on concealed butt hinges.

The London Building Acts of the late 18th century discouraged the use of projecting timberwork which was replaced in the capital, and later elsewhere, by a more ornate treatment of brick and stone surrounds, although throughout the 18th and 19th century many everyday houses stuck with simple square-headed doors.

Fanlights were another development seen in Queen Anne and Georgian times, while the end of the 18th century saw the increasing use of open ornamental cast iron porches, often added to older homes. Stone, or mock stone, porches with classical columns were common in late 18th and early 19th terraced town houses.

A note of caution on relying too much on door styles for dating: since the door is a focus of attention, owners often up-graded it using the current styles and the house may in fact be much older.

Door styles:

A 15th century plank and ledge door.

An 18th century Georgian classical style door.

A mid Victorian door.

For more information on door styles see pp 126–134)

Local Records for Dating Houses

To pinpoint accurately the date of a particular house local records can be very useful. It can also be fun to discover who has lived in a particular house. The starting point for searching for information is the local County Record Office relating to the site of the house.

County Records Offices hold much of the material needed for detailed inquiries of this kind. The most important are:

Ordnance Survey Maps

These can position the house exactly and it is possible to tell if the house has been renumbered or the street renamed since it was built.

Tithe Maps

When church tithes were changed to an annual charge in 1840, a map was produced showing the divisions of parish land in numbered portions. The numbers relate to an accompanying Tithe Apportionment which lists the amount of land allotted to these numbers together with information about the owners and their status.

Rate Books

Most County Record Offices keep a card index showing when areas were first rated. By diligent searching it is possible to determine when a property was first built and who has lived in it since.

Other valuable sources of information usually kept by County Record Offices include:
Electoral Registers
Census Returns
Street Directories
Land Tax Returns
Estate Records
Borough Records

The majority of County Record Offices also keep a card index of properties which detail anything known about them. Many C.R.O.s keep a list of the names of people featured in documents in their possession such as wills and leases.

The archivist at the County Record Office is the best person to advise on how to get the most out of the wealth of information held there.

Bibliography

AISLED TIMBER HALLS AND RELATED BUILDINGS, *C. A. Hewitt*, Transactions of the Ancient Monuments Society, 1976

BRITISH HISTORICAL ROOF-TYPES AND THEIR MEMBERS: A CLASSIFICATION, *R. A. Cordingly*, Transactions of the Ancient Monuments Society, 1961

BUILDING STONES OF ENGLAND AND WALES, *Norman Davey*, Standing Conference for local history, 1976

THE CARE OF OLD BUILDINGS TODAY, *Donald Insall*, Architectural Press, 1972

CHIMNEYS IN OLD BUILDINGS, *G. B. A. Williams*, S.P.A.B., 1976

DISCOVERING TIMBER-FRAMED BUILDINGS, *Richard Harris*, Shire, 1978

ENGLISH COTTAGES AND SMALL FARMHOUSES, *Paul Oliver*, Arts Council, 1975

THE ENGLISH COUNTRY COTTAGE, *R. J. Brown*, Robert Hale, 1979

THE ENGLISH FARMHOUSE AND COTTAGE, *M. W. Bailey*, Routledge and Keegan Paul, 1961

THE ENGLISH HOME, *H. E. Priestley*, Muller, 1971

THE FAMILY HOUSE IN ENGLAND, *Andrew Henderson*, Phoenix House, 1964

GEORGIAN HOUSES FOR ALL, *John Woodforde*, Routledge and Keegan Paul, 1978

GUIDE TO WESTERN ARCHITECTURE, *John Gloag*, George Allen and Unwin, 1958

THE HOUSE AND COTTAGE HANDBOOK, *Neville Whittaker*, Civic Trust for North East, 1976

HOW OLD IS YOUR HOUSE?, *Pamela Cunnington*, Alpha, Books 1980

THE IDEA OF THE VILLAGE, *Gillian Darley*, Arts Council, 1976

ILLUSTRATED HANDBOOK OF VERNACULAR ARCHITECTURE, *R. W. Brunskill*, Faber, 1970

MEDIEVAL ENGLAND, *Colin Platt*, Routledge and Keegan Paul, 1978

OLD ENGLISH HOUSES, *Hugh Braun*, Faber, 1962

ON THE DATING OF ENGLISH HOUSES FROM EXTERNAL EVIDENCE, *J. T. Smith and E. M Yates*, Field Studies, 1968

AN OUTLINE OF EUROPEAN ARCHITECTURE, *Nikolaus Pevsner*, Penguin, (revised 1968)

PICTORIAL HISTORY OF ENGLISH ARCHITECTURE, *John Betjeman*, John Murray, 1972

THE SHELL BOOK OF COTTAGES, *Richard Reid*, Micheal Joseph, 1977

THE SMALLER ENGLISH HOUSE, *Lyndon Cave*, Hale, 1981

THE STORY OF WESTERN ARCHITECTURE, *Bill Risebero*, Herbert Press, 1979

STRENGTHENING TIMBER FLOORS, *John MacGregor*, S.P.A.B., 1973

TIMBER FRAMED BUILDINGS, *Richard Harris*, Arts Council, 1980

THE TIMBER FRAMED HOUSE IN ENGLAND, *Trudy West*, David and Charles

TRADITIONAL BUILDINGS OF BRITAIN, *R. W. Brunskill*, Victor Gollancz, 1981

UNDERSTANDING TOWNS, *David Stenhouse*, Wayland, 1977

THE VILLAGE GREEN, *Paul Oliver*, Arts Council

YOUR COUNTRY COTTAGE, *Robert Edmunds*, David and Charles, 1970

YOUR HOUSE: THE OUTSIDE VIEW, *John Prizeman*, Hutchinson, 1975

Index